A LONG SILENCE

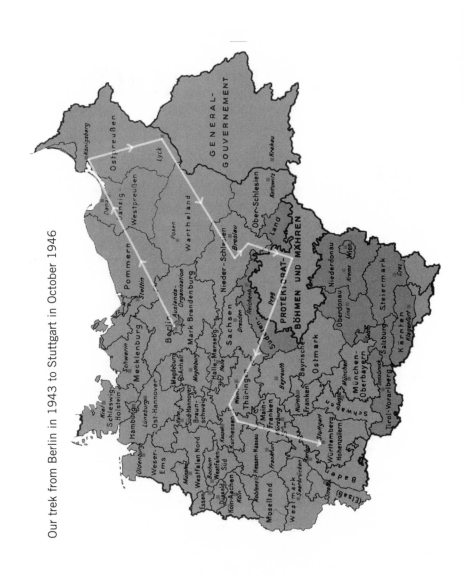

Our trek from Berlin in 1943 to Stuttgart in October 1946

SABINA
DE WERTH
NEU

A LONG SILENCE

MEMORIES OF A GERMAN
REFUGEE CHILD, 1941-1958

 Prometheus Books
59 John Glenn Drive
Amherst, New York 14228–2119

Published 2011 by Prometheus Books

Cover background image © 2004 Dover Publications, Inc.

Inquiries should be addressed to
Prometheus Books
59 John Glenn Drive
Amherst, New York 14228–2119
VOICE: 716–691–0133
FAX: 716–691–0137
WWW.PROMETHEUSBOOKS.COM

15 14 13 12 11   5 4 3 2 1

Library of Congress Cataloging-in-Publication Data

Neu, Sabina de Werth, 1941–
    A long silence : memories of a German refugee child, 1941–1958 / by Sabina de Werth Neu.
        p. cm.
    ISBN 978–1–61614–256–8 (pbk. : alk. paper)
    1. Neu, Sabina de Werth, 1941– 2. World War, 1939–1945—Children—Germany.
3. World War, 1939–1945—Personal narratives, German. 4. Children and war—
Germany. 5. Children—Germany—Biography. 6. Refugees—Germany—Biography.
7. Germany—Biography. I. Title.

D810.C4N48 2011
940.53092—dc22
[B]   2010043644

Printed in the United States of America on acid-free paper

In Memoriam

To my mother, Klarissa (1911–1992)
and my sister Kristina (1938–1981)

To the American people
for their immense
generosity of heart

SOURCES AND PERMISSIONS

CHAPTER 11

"Waking" from *Where Many Rivers Meet* by David Whyte (1955–). Printed with permission from Many Rivers Press, www.davidwhyte.com. 1990 © Many Rivers Press, Langley, Washington.

CHAPTER 12

Japanese haiku by Karo, from *The Four Seasons: Japanese Haiku by Bashō Matsuo*. Peter Pauper Press, Inc., 202 Mamaroneck Ave., Suite 300, White Plains, NY 10601-5376. www.peterpauper.com. Phone: (914) 681-0144. Fax: (914) 681-0389. E-mail: customerservice@peterpauper.com.

CHAPTER 17

"The Lightest Touch" by David Whyte (1955–). Printed with permission from Many Rivers Press, www.davidwhyte.com. From *Everything Is Waiting for You*, 2003 © Many Rivers Press, Langley, Washington.

ACKNOWLEDGMENTS

The support and affection of many people throughout my life have made it possible for me to come to this place where I can finally break the silence and tell the story of my early years, a story that has been lived in one way or another by millions of civilians caught up in the trauma and destruction of wars.

I thank them all, teachers, friends, and the policy makers of the Marshall Plan. But there are some who deserve a special mention: the family of Hans and Udi Stingele, who opened their house to refugee children; my therapist, Brick McDill, who, during the early 1990s, helped me to uncover the trauma of those years; my mentor and teacher, Professor Dr. Jack Childs, who introduced me to Dr. Poldi Orlando, a depth-psychologist, under whose guidance I discovered my own voice and the courage to express myself; the late Carol Alwell, who saw only good in me and urged me to write; Newport friends Kay Parent and Joanne Nelson; Miami friends Nicholas Pisaris and Anja Vie; and so many others.

Special thanks go to the visionary David Whyte, writer of prose and powerful poetry that poses "questions that have no right to go away." During a weeklong workshop with him in the English Lake District in 2006, a fire was lit in my soul. Within a few days of my return, this memoir was flowing out of me like molten lava that had finally risen to the surface into the clean air of my adult life.

I want to thank the novelists Larry McMurtry and Tucker Malarkey, as well as Edward Wates of Blackwell Publishing in Oxford, England, who all read the manuscript and suggested ways to deepen and improve it.

ACKNOWLEDGMENTS

My agent, Gerry McCauley, of McCauley Agency, who believed in my work and left no stone unturned to place it with the right publisher, deserves my special thanks.

And finally, thanks go to my editor, Mark G. Hall, at Prometheus Books, who not only steered me through the publishing process but gave me the gift of his deep understanding and empathy, while editing the manuscript with amazing skill and enthusiasm.

The greatest encouragement came from my beloved husband, Charles. His love and understanding, his extraordinary emotional perception created a safe environment during our fifteen years together. Because of him, I now own, without shame or guilt, my entire life.

Sabina de Werth Neu, Miami, Florida, 2010

PREFACE

In May 1996, on a visit to a friend's farm near Leesburg, Virginia, I found myself across the street from Dodona Mansion, the beloved former home of George C. Marshall, the architect of the Marshall Plan. I wandered over with my husband-to-be, a diplomatic historian of the twentieth century, Charles E. Neu, and found myself in the Visitors Center, watching a documentary about the great general and statesman.

The effect of seeing this man, who had played such a life-giving role in all of Europe and in particular in my young life as a German refugee child, was overwhelming. Tears washed down my face, my chest heaved with joy and gratitude as I heard his voice, saw him move, walk, and smile. He had not been a figment of my imagination after all. He was right there in the little room, the man I had, in my childish ways, adopted as my uncle, someone in all the confusion of my circumstances I could rely on and trust.

I was so undone that I begged one of the staff to let me go into the mansion, which at that time was unrestored and in a bad state. The staff member, to whom I could explain only little between new waves of deep emotion and tears, seemed to understand and she allowed me to go through the muddy grounds into the house. She showed me the general's favorite room and the leather chair he had always sat in. Before I knew what I was doing, I was sitting in it.

What happened next is difficult to describe. A rush of love, grief, and old longing enveloped me. It came to me that this great man had been like a father to me and had watched over me my whole life. I felt his presence in the room. Sitting there felt like a kind of homecoming. At that moment I knew that I was finally going to write about my family's World War II and postwar experiences. I was being flooded by memories of my life in Germany as a small child. I totally understood how my faith in this nearly mythical figure had helped me through the trials of my small life. Marshall's practical and humanitarian programs had saved my ailing body and soul. And here I was in his America, with my Charles, who loved and understood me. How blessed my life had been, despite everything.

The years since 1977, when I came to the United States, were the first years I'd felt safe from war or impending war. During the cold war years in Europe there was always the eerie threat and possibility of Russian missiles annihilating all of us. Somehow I felt safe from all that in the big, powerful United States of America, which was so far away.

By 1982 I had become a citizen. Two years later, I left my English husband and started a new life in the land of possibilities. I drove cross-country and ended up working for the US Forest Service for three years as a lowly GS-2 (there are fifteen "General Schedule" grades in the federal government employment system). But I had wanted to give something back to the country, which had been so generous to us, by "protecting the land and serving the people" (the motto of the US Forest Service). At the same time, I entered long-term therapy with a very gifted psychologist and was able to work through the traumas from my early life. This lifted the heavy shroud of occasional deep depressions off me. When I returned to Rhode Island, I was ready to finish my interrupted degree in psychology, and eventually I became an effective therapist.

When Charles walked into my life, or I into his, I was blossoming. I was writing on and off, mostly short stuff and some poetry. Then, in the summer of 2006, after a poetry workshop and walking tour in the English Lake District, under the guidance of the marvelous poet and visionary David Whyte, I was finally on fire and ready to tell my story.

One of the greatest surprises I've experienced while writing these memoirs was learning how the human memory works. Of course I had the outline of my early experiences through things my mother had told us and what my sister Gabriele remembered, like places, names, and the chronology of events. But the greatest help were the many photographs that had survived, the tiny black-and-white prints over which I would sit with a magnifying glass for hours. Often one small thing in the picture would trigger a whole episode, or some feelings and smells, and before I knew it I was right there in the moment. As though in a sort of trance or self-hypnosis I could follow the events, see the episodes as if I was watching a 3-D film with all the sensations and feelings. For instance, while I was looking intently at the picture of myself at age three in a sandbox in East Prussia, I suddenly saw a figure coming through the grass. It was the forester whom Mother once mentioned to us in later years. I saw him from his boots up and was fascinated by the three horn buttons on his jacket. And so one thing would lead to another.

I believe we remember all the high points and the low points in our emotional memory. I wrote the first draft in six weeks, as if in a fever. I was afraid that the connection to my childhood would suddenly be unplugged. But it never happened. Looking back at my childhood and adolescence now is very different; the lines have been straightened out. There is a clarity and spaciousness about it all, so much so that I don't just feel lighter, I actually feel taller.

This book is my thank you to the American people for their kindness, generosity, and the sacrifices they made during those hard postwar years in Europe. It is also a small expression of my enormous gratitude for all those, led by George Marshall, who implemented the recovery plan. I am here because of those enlightened human beings. I hope this small book can remind the reader, during these very difficult times in America, that what was possible then is possible now, under responsible and truly compassionate leadership. The world needs you, America.

Truth is never absolute, neither is memory; both have so many layers. After writing the first draft, rereading the manuscript, and listening to the questions of some of the people who had read it, I realized that I had to break the long silence, my own and that of many of my contemporaries. I needed to speak about what it was like for some of us to grow up during and immediately after the Nazi era. So much still lay hidden deep inside and had to be pried open, like old, moldy trunks in deep, dank basements.

I am German—there, I have said it. I can never be anything else. I have been hiding from this burdensome truth for most of my life and running from the nightmare of a war and the industrialized barbarism of an evil regime that I could not and did not want to accept, let alone try to understand.

Instead I became a master of disguise, never being the same person for very long, creating new parts and pasts for myself—anything not to be German. In my thirties I even rolled the year of my birth forward by ten years. It sounded so much better and did not connect me as closely to the Hitler years. However, by denying the most formative ten years of my personal history, I became a half person, cutting away the foundation of why I was the way I was, and putting myself in danger of collapsing altogether. Denial is a dangerous and destructive force.

All that is behind me now; the German in me has been let out. I have lived in self-imposed exile for forty-five years, first in England and now in the United States of America.

When the English translation of Günther Grass's *Peeling the Onion* was published and widely reviewed, I was emboldened. The title of his recent memoir fascinated me. His metaphor of peeling the onion was so close to my own simple reminiscences. During my months of writing, I had been reminded again and again of eating an artichoke, taking off, one by one, the outer leaves, which were rigid, had sharp thorns, and yielded little to no nourishment at their other end. But I continued and came closer to the middle, where the leaves became more tender, more succulent, more life-sustaining. Then I reached the chalice, protected by hundreds of hairy pustules, which, when removed, allowed me to eat the entire vessel, including the stem.

This is how I experienced writing this book. The first third was like the outer leaves, hard and fraught with danger, producing a gnawing hunger. In later chapters, when I came to the fuzzy part, instead of looking deeper, trying to understand it, I removed it with a knife, amputating it, just as I had tried to cut away my shame and guilt. I fled into silence, where those feelings would fester and rot, invading the very essence of my being. But eventually I had to give it up; I was so tired of hiding in the dark. I had to become visible. The process of ingesting the bitter fruit of memory became my private communion, taking my own life and identity into my body.

That is where I found compassion and understanding. I could bring these qualities to Grass's long silence about having briefly served in the Nazi *Waffen* SS (a powerful military unit created by Adolf Hitler) as an adolescent, and over time forgive and comprehend my own muteness.

And yet, my national origin and some of the guilt and shame will always be part of me, like a hump or a clubfoot. How could it be otherwise for a member and survivor of a nation that waged two terrible wars on the world, exterminated six million Jews, and at least three million others—homosexuals, Gypsies, left-wing liberals, the mentally ill and insane, the physically handicapped, and anybody else who did not fit into its leaders' psychopathic and arbitrary Aryan ideals?

I am for better or worse a reluctant German. Many of my contemporaries have to carry a similar burden, each one in its own way, for the rest of our lives. We were the children of monsters, not directly, but by association.

I spent the last four months of 2007 in Washington and by sheer happenstance rented an apartment that was diagonally across from the Center of the German George Marshall Fund of the United States of America and two buildings away from the German Historical Institute, where I attended lectures and had access to an extensive library. It felt as if some force had guided me to this very street. I had the opportunity to meet with enough Germans of my generation to know that many of them have struggled with issues similar to mine, and just as many chose to remain silent about the painful past. They said things like "Too much water has gone under the bridge" or "What is the point of talking about it?" It is the younger generation, especially those born after 1975, that is able to look at the era of World War II as just history and move forward.

Will I ever be a "good German"? I doubt it. I have been away for so long, have spoken a new language, and integrated into two new cultures and societies. In short visits over forty years, I always felt myself falling into a gray and undefined space. Speaking German felt uncomfortable and difficult. Despite my fluency, the change from English to my native language had a bizarre effect on me; my voice would drop lower, and communicating spontaneously became almost impossible. German, I discovered, is a heavy language. It is not so much the syntax or the grammar as the individual words, which are so heavily descriptive. They pulled me back into a more serious, orderly, and humorless world, reminding me of the very things I had tried to escape from. My own subjective experiences made me even shun the wonderful poets and writers of the past. Most words stem from root words and often are constructions of several concepts, but they always carry the timbre and emotional color of the original meaning. No wonder there is no German thesaurus. There seems to be no gray, only black and white. I believe it is part of the German national character.

Being in Washington while rewriting and editing my memoir was a real gift. The Vietnam War Memorial on the National Mall became a place for healing where I could allow the pain, the rage, and all the feelings overwhelming my small body to be flushed out in endless tears, together with the shame and guilt I have carried for so long. I have talked to many Vietnam veterans there, most of them crippled both outside and inside.

This monument, in its abstraction, this deep black scar in the earth with its never-ending list of names, expresses all the loss and futility, the sickness and inhumanity that have marred the record of human history and continue to do so today. As the black marble disappears into the earth, it appears to extend endlessly, penetrating continents, islands, and oceans, and absorbing the hundreds of millions of names of lives cut short on this still beautiful planet.

OPENING

One day the frosted glass
Shattered.
Slowly, quietly,
Falling down
In a mosaic of pieces.

Not a cataclysmic event,
Something just had
To give way.

The world,
Only guessed at,
Kept out
For all those years
Of self-imposed exile,
Rushed in
As I rushed out, blinded,
As wind danced round me,
As rain mingled
With my tears.

Stunned I stood,
Awed, motionless,
Breathing my first
Liberated breath.

I was falling
In love with the
Otherness,
Recognizing it as
All the longing
Of this caged bird,

PREFACE

Finally free,
Taking its place
In pure air.

—Sabina de Werth Neu, June 2006

CHAPTER 1

My mother groan'd, my father wept
Into the dangerous world I lept;
Helpless, naked, piping loud,
Like a fiend hid in a cloud.
— William Blake (1757–1827), "Infant Sorrow"

My mother often told me what a pleasant, cheerful baby I had been. Even my birth was easy, compared to that of my two older sisters, Gabriele and Kristina. I came into this world on September 26, 1941, in Berlin, Nazi Germany.

What a time and place to start life. Bombs were falling on Berlin, sporadically lighting up the night sky, yet they were frequent enough that I had to spend the third night of my young life in an air-raid bunker, next to Haus Dahlem, a private maternity clinic in a residential part of the city. The underground shelter was cold and damp, and I contracted a middle-ear infection. Of course I do not remember this. My mother revealed to me that around the end of September "Der Führer" made a surprise visit to the clinic in order to congratulate all the mothers on their new babies (no doubt Aryan babies). According to my mother, he leaned down over my crib and smiled.

Mother spoke of this when I was a teenager. I was in shock. By then I knew enough about the Third Reich to feel as if I had been touched by Evil early on and that the subsequent suffering must have been a direct result of it, just like the spell cast on Sleeping Beauty by the evil godmother. I felt branded somehow and carried the guilt and shame of it right through adolescence and early adulthood.

Mother with Sabina, Berlin, 1941

Mother and Hertha standing in back with Sabina (in carriage),
Tina (forefront), and Gabi (behind)

Gabi and Tina with new sister Sabina, October 1941

Sabina, Berlin, 1942

SABINA DE WERTH NEU

In Europe in the 1950s many rumors were circulating that Hitler had escaped from Berlin in 1945 and that the charred body outside his bunker was not really his. So, in 1960 during a youth hostel trip, when I saw a man who looked like Hitler in, of all places, Galway, Ireland, I became obsessed with bringing him to justice. I followed him all day, through rain and high winds, from pub to pub, and finally sought the help of a local policeman. He just laughed at me, pointing out "Hitler" as a Galway man named William who wore the short moustache and odd hairstyle to annoy the English, who had taken such a beating during the German bombing of London. Everyone in town thought it was a great joke.

I cannot substantiate my early encounter with Hitler. I have not found any proof that he was in Berlin during that time, but then he often appeared unexpectedly from Austria or East Prussia. The events of the next five years, however, still seem as if someone had cast a devilish curse over us and millions of other people too.

We lived in Berlin. My father had been called up and entered the Luftwaffe (air force). The city continued to be bombed, and my sisters would be picked up in late afternoon, together with many other children, to spend the night in a bomb shelter. We lived in a modest apartment on the Grazer Damm until 1942, when things had become so dangerous that the authorities decided to start a vast evacuation program for mothers with young children. We had already been assigned a young girl called Hertha to help my mother. She was what was then called a *Pflichtjahr Mädchen* (literally, a duty-year girl), straight out of school, as fresh and innocent as "milk and honey," as Mother described her.

My parents and two sisters had moved to Berlin at the beginning of the war, because Father had found work as a buyer for men's clothes for the big department-store chain Karstatt. He had no college education, having been thrown out of his mother's home before he was twenty. My paternal grandmother was very strict and pious; so whatever my father had done, it must have been bad enough in her eyes to disinherit and sever all ties with her youngest son. Mother explained in later years that he was spoiled and wanted the good life but suffered from a weak character, a lack of moral backbone. According to her, he was more inter-ested in entertaining attractive women than in learning and striving to make something of himself.

Serving in the German Luftwaffe was not such a bad position for him. He saw no real action, as he was doing mostly administrative and clerical work due to his very neat handwriting. Apparently he came on leave to Berlin in 1942, but, of course, I have no recollection of this. Mother was glad to get out of our dreary apartment and out of the city, which became increasingly dangerous.

Hitler wanted to preserve the broodmares and offsprings for his Thousand-Year Aryan Reich and still believed that he could hold the front to the east. Tens of thousands were thus moved to the very eastern limits of the country and were subsequently abandoned and forgotten when the Soviet army broke through. Mother had no idea how long this dreadful war would hold us in its grasp or that it would drag us through a large part of Eastern Europe.

CHAPTER 2

East and west on fields forgotten
Bleach the bones of comrades slain,
Lovely lads and dead and rotting,
None that go return again.

—A. E. Housman (1858–1936),
"On the idle hill of summer,"
from *A Shropshire Lad* (1896)

Mother, Hertha, and we three girls were put on one of the many trains heading to the east. We were assigned to travel to East Prussia (today northeast Poland and Russia). The train stopped many times on the seven-hundred-kilometer journey to Königsberg (today Kaliningrad, Russia). Troop trains and trains hauling boxcars, probably filled with the Jewry of northern Europe, sped by, as they had preference to bring their occupants, hundreds of thousands, to their deaths.

We were oblivious to all of this. I happily swung in my hammock-like nest, the lower luggage rack, just above my mother's head. From there I saw everything rushing by, bare trees, other trains, changing late-winter skies, bright lights, chimneys, and hills covered in snow, all to the regular heartbeat of the coal-fed locomotive or the screeching and clanging of the brakes. But mostly I remember being lulled to sleep between feedings at my mother's soft and warm breasts.

On arrival in Königsberg, we changed to a local train, destination Lyck (today Elk, Poland), the county town of one of the many regions of the Masurenland. From there we took a primitive cart drawn by a shire

House in Rundfliess (today Krzywen), Poland, 1942–1944

horse to the small village of Rundfliess (Krzywen). It was built in a circle around one of the smaller of the region's more than 2,700 lakes. The Masuren region was formed during the last ice age. In between the bodies of water are wonderful pastures and huge pine forests, interspersed with birches and some maples. Today it is Poland's vacationland. The first German settlers arrived in the fourteenth century.

It became part of the German Empire in 1871 and was nearly 75 percent German; the rest of the population was Polish and Lithuanian until 1945. In 1939, approximately 2.5 million Germans lived there.

Children in grass, house in background

We were sent to a country estate owned by a family called the Bordins, who were less than enthusiastic to have to give up space to city folks from Berlin and did not treat my mother very well. We were allowed to occupy an apartment on the second floor that had been used as a summer rental before the war. For us children, especially Gabi (born in 1935) and Tina (born in 1938), it was heaven after the restricting life in the middle of a large city. Here they could run around, visit all the animals, horses, goats, geese, and chickens, as well as the still-wintry gardens and the grand yellow house.

But Mother, a young woman of thirty-two, was looking for some-

Gabi, Sabina, and Tina, winter

Tina, Gabi, and Sabina, gymnastics, summer

where else to live where she would not be resented. With her innate charm and willpower, her striking good looks, her statuesque figure and posture—which commanded respect—as well as her expressive dark brown eyes and lilting voice, she somehow managed to convince an official at the town hall to find us a small house for rent at the edge of the village down a dirt road. The one-and-a-half-story house had a large garden and a huge tiled Russian woodstove that heated most of the house. The house was very charming in its simplicity; the fact that it had no electricity and an outhouse near the back door did not dampen Mother's spirit. We would make do with candles, petroleum lamps, and chamber pots for nighttime, and she could cook in the kitchen on a small stove fed by wood. I can't remember how we reached the outhouse during the long snowy winters, but we must have managed somehow. I was unaware of all these inconveniences in our cozy cheerful house.

As soon as all the snow had melted, Mother started a garden with Hertha's help. Neither of them had any experience in gardening, but they sowed vegetable seeds, set potatoes, planted strawberries, and asked a local farmer to come and plant some gooseberry and black-currant bushes and to prune the small neglected apple and pear orchard. It was quite an enterprise, undertaken with much laughter and singing.

One day, Mother pulled a small black-and-white fox terrier out of her large shopping bag. We called him Pucki, and later on a brown German dachshund adopted us.

We kept rabbits and chickens, and in early summer we went through the woods picking wild raspberries, which Mother made into delicious preserves. It became one of her favorite things to do for the rest of her life. She delighted her friends and us with pretty jars of all kinds of reminders of the bounty of summer right up until her death in 1992.

The previous owners had built a lovely sandpit in the garden, and I spent much of my time in it. Today I feel uneasy when I think of the people who had lived there before us, leaving behind their simple furniture and other belongings. Had they left voluntarily (unlikely) or

Tina and Sabina with dachshund

Sabina, Gabi, and Tina by lakefront

were they taken by force to perish in one of the killing places of which there were so many? I feel guilty now that we had such a wonderfully happy time there all together, a time that could never be repeated in our future lives and that was perhaps the result of others dying so we could live there.

Mother had turned into something of a pioneer woman. She had inherited her sharp common sense and practical ability from her father, who had been a jack-of-all-trades. When our furniture arrived from Berlin, she was dancing, laughing, and crying all at the same time. Her manual sewing machine was her prized possession, and she immediately set it up. Then a frenzy of activity began: buying fabric in the town of Lyck and sewing curtains, pillowcases, lampshades, tablecloths, and beautifully smocked dresses for her three daughters. I assume that the money for rent and our living expenses came from Father's military pay.

It is amazing to me that we could have lived so close to the fighting in Russia, so close to Hitler's fortress, the *Wolfsschanze* (wolf's lair), only sixty miles away, near Rastenberg. But the German bureaucratic machinery was still working well. Furniture could be sent, money transferred, the mail functioned, but we had no news as to what was happening, no radio or newspapers. So we were lulled into a false sense of relative security. Mother had obviously settled in as if she were going to live in Rundfliess for many years to come and seemed quite happy about it. The mail brought news from her two siblings, her brother, Kurt, who was a noncommissioned officer on the eastern front, and her younger sister, Marga, who was in Silesia. *Onkel* (Uncle) Kurt visited us in our rural paradise more than once during his furloughs, and most of the photos he took of us survived because Mother sent the rolls of film to *Tante* (Aunt) Marga, who worked in a photographer's studio. I vaguely recall *Onkel* Kurt; he played with us, and his musical laughter filled house and garden. He had the same beautiful brown eyes as my mother.

Looking at the photographs today I see my sister Tina's face, so radiant, the way it would never shine again throughout her remaining life. We were living in some kind of bubble. I was chasing the white

Children reading with *Onkel* Kurt

Mother with her three girls

geese along the lake's edge in the summer, and in the snowy winter of 1943–44 my sisters pulled me on a sled through a white magical world of pristine snow.

And that Christmas, Mother drilled me to recite a German *Weihnacht's* (Christmas) poem, something about a child meeting the little Christ child in the snow-covered woods. I must have been like a little parrot as I learned all the intonations, facial expressions, and movements, and I was a great success at the local church's Christmas feast, where my strong lisp only enhanced my precocious performance. To this day I remember some of the lines.

We had a record snowfall that winter. The snow reached the second-story windows, and we mainly lived and slept downstairs like hibernating mice around the big woodstove. Mother and Hertha taught us songs and read fairy stories to us to pass the time. Then one day there were voices outside. Some local people had come to check on us and dig us out, and they had brought fresh bread and milk.

After that the mud season started. Our road was not paved, and I often fell headlong into the mud. Mother believed in the therapeutic effect of fresh air, and we were outside as much as possible, no matter what the weather was like. I have no idea how she and Hertha managed to keep us clean, having to wash everything by hand, but they did.

With the great thaw came the spring flowers, and I learned, now being two and a half and very active, how to make daisy and buttercup chains for myself and everyone. Later, the songbirds returned and horse carriages drove up and down our road. One day a boy told me to pick up one of the horse droppings, which he said were really "horse apples" (*PferdeÄpfel*) and very good to eat. They were still steaming in the cool air, but I bent down to get one and took a bite. The texture was prickly and difficult to chew and tasted nothing like an apple from a tree. My sister Gabi came running, chased the boy away, and dragged me home so Mother could clean out my mouth and the rest of me. Everyone laughed and thought it was so funny, but I could not see the humor in it.

We had not heard anything about *Onkel* Kurt for quite a while, and Mother grew anxious. People said the war was not going so well.

A LONG SILENCE

Meeting Father in Westpreussen

Sabina in sandbox   Sabina, mud season, 1944

Around the end of May, Mother got a letter from the Luftwaffe. My father had been injured in a fluke accident on a truck and was in a *Lazarett* (military hospital) somewhere in West Prussia. We all took a train to see him. There exists a picture of him in pajamas holding me in one arm and kissing me on the mouth, which I remember not liking very much. I had no real connection to him and only noticed that he did not smell as nice as *Onkel* Kurt.

Back in Rundfliess all appeared peaceful. No one talked about the invasion by the allied forces on the beaches of Normandy in June 1944 or the attempted assassination on Hitler by Colonel Claus von Stauffenberg on July 20, less than sixty miles to the northwest of us. And no one really believed that the Russians were advancing in the southeast or fighting "next door" in Lithuania.

As we children were getting older—I was then nearly three, my sisters six and nine—we did not need Hertha any longer. She was terribly homesick and worried about her parents in Berlin, so she left us one bright summer morning. We all cried and waved long after the horse and cart had disappeared around a corner. We would never see her again and would never know what happened to her. After the war, Mother tried for a long time to find her, but to no effect. It was as if she had disappeared from the face of the earth, like so many millions of others.

Mother had befriended a nice older man, the local forester, on one of our wild raspberry-picking forays into the surrounding woods. I think he was maybe a bit in love with my rather exotic and beautiful young mother. Anyhow, he would stop by quite often, bringing a wild hare, some fruit, and even a load of firewood, as well as bunches of wildflowers. We girls loved these visits. He was fun to play with and could build wonderful sand castles in our sandbox. Pucki, the terrier, would, unfortunately, dive nose first into them and destroy the fanciful creations. I can't recall the forester's name, but I can still see him coming through the garden in his knee breeches, boots, and dark green jacket with big buttons.

Onkel Kurt, 1937

Tante Marga and *Onkel* Kurt, 1943

In my teenage years, Mother told me in a moment of self-revelation that she had been very fond of our man in green and even had fantasies that we would stay in East Prussia and he would be our new father. I gathered that my parents' marriage had already been shaky before I was born, because I was conceived during a brief reconciliation over the Christmas holidays in 1940.

Who knows what might have happened had not the Russians advanced slowly from the southeast, giving us just enough time to make preparations to get out. The kind forester must have given my mother some warning, as he wanted us to get out of harm's way. So Mother started making little piles and packages, packing and unpacking, checking weight, taking things out or completely repacking. It was very confusing, and I seemed forever to be in her way. All three of us felt her anxiety fill the whole house. It was now the middle of October 1944 and getting colder, and the small village was talking about the Red Army only weeks away in Lithuania, where *Onkel* Kurt was fighting.

We were frightened. The forester came nearly every day. One day in late October he took us to Lyck to be put on a transport by train heading southwest. The station was full of women with children, and soon we were saying tearful good-byes to our savior. We would never see or hear from him again.

Omi and her beloved Kurt,
during the war

Onkel Kurt on furlough from the front,
five months before he died

CHAPTER 3

The stars are dead.
The animals will not look.
We are left alone with our day
And the time is short
And history to the defeated
May say alas but cannot help or pardon.

—W. H. Auden (1907–1973), "Spain 1937"

My memory of the first part of our journey from East Prussia is quite hazy. The train was overcrowded and reeked of urine. The smell of fear and the dark sorrow of having to leave everything one loved behind—animals, the vast forests and gentle lakes, old friends, and all one's possessions—enveloped everyone like a black shroud.

Mother had two medium-sized bulging suitcases, and we three girls each carried a backpack. Mine had a special hook in the back from which a small white enamel chamber pot dangled. Gabi had insisted on taking her large doll, which she would clutch for the next few months. She still has this doll now, at age seventy-one, and recently bought her a set of new clothes. Maybe she has finally made peace with the past.

The train moved slowly, often stopping for long periods on some sidetrack, while overcrowded troop trains were speeding by, heading west. We had to change trains often, sometimes waiting many days in a dirty station or a primitive camp, a school, or other public buildings, sleeping on cold floors. It was now bitterly cold outside; food was scarce and difficult to distribute for the many thousands of refugees. In the German language we were *Flüchtlinge*, literally "people in flight," or "flee-lings." We were fleeing from something and had no idea what kind of refuge, if any, was ahead of us. But when news reached us in January 1945 that the Russian army had cut off East Prussia from the German Reich, we were glad to have escaped in time.

The ones who did not get out in time could only flee across the Baltic Sea, some on foot over the now frozen sea toward Finland, many perishing on the way. Others tried to get out on ships that could cut through the ice, only to be torpedoed by the Russian navy. And yet, two million managed to escape right up to the end of the war in May 1945, some to Sweden, others to Denmark. Many of the remaining Germans were slaughtered by the Red Army in the cruelest ways or deported to die slowly in the Siberian labor camps.

We were safe for the time being. Food was constantly on our minds. In some small towns, where the train stopped, people had set up soup kitchens on the train platforms, where they served lentils in a gray liquid, hot potatoes, and maybe pieces of bread. The cold was our biggest enemy; the heating only worked when the train was moving, but we managed to huddle together. Mother was an avid reader and knew so much despite having had to leave school at age fourteen. She would tell us made-up stories about three brave little girls who went on adventurous journeys to the far corners of the world. We couldn't get enough of her stories, the main purpose of which was to keep our minds off our immediate surroundings.

Often the train would be split up in sections, some cars going more west, others more to the southwest. We were finally unloaded in what was then called Böhmen and Mähren, the former Czechoslovakia, in a town called Zwittau (now Svitavy), to the east of Prague. Zwittau, Oskar Schindler's birthplace, had a population of about ten thousand, mostly German. We did not see much of the medieval town with its many churches because we were transported to the outskirts and placed on a large farm in a place called Vierzig Huben.

Once again, luck was with us. A family of tenant farmers, named Friedel, took an instant liking to us, and so once again we were able to stay in a vacation apartment. The Friedels fed us well; there was an endless supply of fresh eggs with orange yolks, thick, creamy milk, honey, and wonderful fresh bread. It must have been early spring by then, as the ground had started to thaw, and it took all the balance I had at the age of three and a half years to negotiate the wooden boards across the muddy farmyard to the big outhouse, to sit on the lowest part of the wooden bench over the smallest hole to do my business. Sometimes my sisters would join me, and we sat next to each other, like three organ pipes, giggling and talking in the communal outhouse. Inside was a stack of cut-up newspapers, which doubled as toilet paper and was also useful for chasing away the ever-present flies.

We also had fun with the farmhands, who liked having young children around and let us play in the hayloft. We built caves out of hay and played hide-and-seek. Father and Mother Friedel seemed quite old and had several sons who had been in the army; some were killed and two were missing in action.

It appeared as if spring had arrived overnight; green grass was sprouting and thousands of dandelions shot up in every conceivable place. Behind one of the barns a narrow footpath led down to a small stream. I was not allowed to go there by myself, but I did it at least once and got a big surprise. Being absorbed in crossing the water, spanning my short legs from rock to rock, afraid of falling in, I suddenly came up to a huge grayish-brown animal, so close to me that I could not see either end of it. I ran back, splashing through the water, screaming in fear, and when I had calmed down somewhat I told everyone that I had nearly walked into an elephant down by the river. They all laughed, including my mother and sisters. But for years afterward I insisted that I really had a close encounter with an elephant and that he must have escaped from a circus.

The farmer's father, a wizened and incredibly wrinkled man, who always sat in the large farm kitchen next to the window, suddenly died one day. The family put his coffin in the big, poorly lit entrance hall, which one had to cross on the way outdoors or to the kitchen. It was spooky for my sisters, knowing the old man was lying in a black box with no air. So, of course, I felt scared too.

A LONG SILENCE

On the day of the funeral, one of the farmhands played a joke on us. As we passed the coffin that morning, a whitish hand and arm seemed to be reaching out for us, ready to grab anyone who passed too close. We children were convinced that the farmer was not really dead and was trying to get out of his box. This made the burial that afternoon even creepier as we stood at the graveside behind the village church. It was particularly gruesome to hear shovel after shovel of reddish clay drop on the coffin while the priest read a very long prayer, including the words "suffered under Pontius Pilatus." Not being familiar with that name, I understood him to say, "suffered under Pompes and Lates," whom I believed were the scoundrels who had killed the old man.

The rest of that spring was lovely. We played outside whenever the weather permitted, drank warm milk straight from the cow, watched cheeses being made, and played with pieces of bread dough in the kitchen when the weather was wet. Radishes and early lettuce could be picked in the vegetable garden, and sometimes for our Sunday meal a fat chicken would sacrifice itself for our enjoyment, or so I thought.

It is amazing to me now that we had come upon such a wonderful refuge, displaced as we were, with people who were so generous, kind, and embracing. We felt relatively safe on this farm, away from the miseries of the cities, living in a kind of cocoon.

Those months at the Friedels' farm may well have been crucial in giving us the strength to survive what was to come.

CHAPTER 4

Still falls the rain—
Dark as the world of man,
Black as our loss—
Blind as the nineteen hundred
And forty nails on the Cross.
Still falls the rain.
— Edith Sitwell (1887–1961), "Still Falls the Rain" (1942)

At midnight May 8, 1945, the complete capitulation of the German *Wehrmacht* (army) was in effect. The next morning hundreds of half-starved and wounded German soldiers came running down the road from the east in small disorganized groups, some stopping for any food they could grab but too terrified to stop for long. Something horrendous seemed to chase them. Mother was glad that this awful war was over at last. None of us knew that for us it was just beginning.

That night, Mother was in our small bedroom, kissing us good night as she did every evening. I was in the top bunk, Tina was below me, and Gabi was in the single bed across the linoleum floor. Mother was just about to leave to go into her bedroom, when we heard the deafening sound of engines, then men's loud voices, breaking of glass, gunshots, drunken singing and shouting, and the loud trampling of boots coming up the stairs. Mother was at the door, deathly pale. She went outside, carefully closing the door behind her. I heard her voice and also loud male laughing. Mother's voice grew fainter, as she led the men away from us.

A LONG SILENCE

We lay motionless in our beds, hardly daring to breathe. It was much quieter for a while. Then the footsteps returned; there must have been so many men out there. I hid under the olive-gray horse blanket and tried not to make a sound.

The door crashed open. Someone smashed the mirror above the marble-top washstand; the sound of the falling glass was strangely comforting. Gabi and Tina were whimpering and then shrieking. I was invisible; no one could find me.

But rough hands did find my feet and pulled me out of bed. I hung upside down, my small white nightie over my head. I was thrown around, and I expected to fall on the hard floor. Something entered between my legs, sharp and thick. The pain was almost unbearable. I wanted to shriek but could not make a sound. All my senses were sharpened. I saw muddy boots; smelled the ogres' sweat and my own blood running through the nightie from my belly to my chin. Tina was crying out in unimaginable terror, like an animal. Everything was happening so slowly.

My nightie was ripped off me; I was tossed again. Something really awful entered my mouth. It was hot and smelled so bad it made me gag. I couldn't breathe. I was dying. *Mutti*, where are you? I was drowning in foul-tasting liquid, suffocating. My face, my ears, my hair was covered with this stuff. The voices were frantic now, spewing words I did not understand. The stench of human excretions was nauseating. I dared not vomit. My stomach was a rock. I could not open my eyes. I was limp, like a lifeless doll, and I was dead. If I was already dead, nothing would hurt me again. I suddenly understood the meaning of "suffered under Pompes and Lates." I fell on the floor. I was picked up, someone laughed, Tina whimpered, I couldn't hear Gabi. Suddenly I heard nothing at all. I was gone.

In the morning at daybreak our mother found us lying in a huddle. Her face was completely swollen and encrusted in blood. She could hardly stand up and limped when she moved. She explained to us that she had fallen in the barn, but as she held and rocked us, she assured us that the Russian soldiers were gone and that everything would be all right.

From then on the world appeared to be in a fog. We had all been broken open like robin's eggs, like the light blue ones I had found under a birch tree just a few weeks earlier. Now everything was in black and white. I was singing to myself, softly. Nothing mattered. I had died and no one could hurt me ever again.

We did not talk about that endless night for many years, and never together. We were pretending that it could not have happened, and we all paid a high price for our silence and denial, in different ways.

CHAPTER 5

History is a nightmare
From which I am trying to awake.
—James Joyce (1882–1941), *Ulysses* (1922)

The farm was in ruins. Farmer Friedel and his wife had been killed and most of the farmhands were missing. Nearly all the animals had been shot dead; only a few chickens were running around in dismay.

Someone came by a few days later with a horse and cart and drove us into the town of Zwittau (Svitavy). There we waited for several weeks in an abandoned factory for a train transport westward. I have no clear recollection of those weeks; there seemed to be just a grayness, as if all the blood had left my veins, all the color was gone out of life, and nothing mattered but the next shallow breath.

Today I know that Zwittau was quite a lovely town, founded in the thirteenth century, with many beautiful buildings. It had belonged to the Holy Roman Empire of the German nation until 1806. For us it was a holding pen, a kind of purgatory, before the next episode of our long escape to the west.

Finally, at the beginning of July 1945, we were allowed on an organized transport, probably arranged by the Czechs or Soviets. At the time I did not know that Germans were forcibly expelled from what now was again Poland and Czechoslovakia, which meant all the inhabitants from the Sudetenland had to leave or be killed. Again, we were the lucky ones. Our train consisted of open wooden cattle cars, the floors still covered with dried manure. The authorities pushed up to eighty people into each car, with very little luggage allowed. We did not manage to get a place against a wall and sat somewhere in the middle on a suitcase and cloth that Mother had spread out. The long reddish-brown doors were rolled shut with a hellish metal screech, and we were off.

That first day we were hardly out of town before the train stopped. We sat in the summer heat, through a wild thunderstorm with hail, eating some of our bread and drinking water. Mother had packed her red-and-black-checkered collapsible umbrella, and it provided shelter from the sun, rain, and the sparks of the coal-fired locomotive when the train was moving. The umbrella also gave us some privacy from the other refugees, creating a little make-believe world of our own. After dark the train moved again, and there was a palpable feeling of optimism and relief. People talked and even laughed together. But before long, we stopped again, trapped in our open coffin, for the rest of the night.

For the 220 miles to the town of Gera, in Thuringia, it took nine days and nine nights. We were stuck in this smelly box with scores of people, no real toilet, just a large bucket, which was difficult to reach and soon overflowed. The water ran out on the third day; the bread had long been eaten; there was no way to wash or change a baby's diapers.

They would not let us out in any of the towns we passed. We felt as if we were carrying the plague. A few times during the nine days and nine nights the train would stop at a river. Train personnel opened the heavy doors just wide enough for four people to get through at a time, and we could walk down to the riverbank for five minutes to wash and fill whatever container we had with river water. My little chamber pot came in handy, and Mother pulled one of her prized wedding gifts out of the suitcase, a sterling silver coffeepot, to fill with water. Nobody cared about the brown color of the water or the sight of dead animals—cattle, dogs, and rats—floating downstream. It was either this or die of thirst, as we had no idea how long this journey would last. When the waste bucket was emptied, the stench made us nearly pass out. A sharp whistle blew, and we all scrambled back into our hellish refuge. The locomotive hissed and sent black steam over us, the brakes were released with a lot of clanging, and we were moving again.

Some mothers' babies had died, and the smell of death was terrible in the summer heat, but the poor distraught women could not part from their little ones without a proper burial. It was as if the living and the dead were condemned together in this high-walled coffin with no lid. People became sick and weaker by the day, my sweet sister Tina among them. Her hands were sweaty, her breathing fast and frantic, and her eyes were glazed and had a faraway look. We were frightened that we'd lose her. Our thirst and hunger hurt. The train stopped in the town of Gera, in the new East Germany. We could see the sign above us.

Everyone who had some strength left banged on the doors and shouted for help, Mother included. She knew that one more day of the stench, the heat, and the lack of food would kill Tina. The door was rolled back, and Gabi and I stumbled out. A big man carried Tina in his arms, and Mother followed with our pitiful luggage.

We had gotten as far west as we could at that point. We were the lucky ones. Millions of European Jews, Gypsies, and other "undesirables" had been making a similar journey, in similar trains, in the opposite direction, only to end up in Hitler's death camps, from which so very few emerged alive. At least we had hope. No one was trying to exterminate us.

CHAPTER 6

Hunger allows no choice
To the citizen or the police;
We must love one another or die.
> —W. H. Auden (1907–1973), "Sept. 1, 1939" (1940)

Some kind soul took us to a nearby school, named after Martin Luther. Mother made a pallet on the floor for us. We received hot boiled potatoes and turnips and as much clean water as we wanted. We ate and drank until our bellies hurt and could hold no more, except for Tina who could hardly swallow anything and fell into a deep sleep. Two women dragged in a mattress for her, and she was carefully lifted onto it, her arms and legs dangling like a rag doll, her brown hair stuck to her sweating face. I was so afraid that she would die.

The next morning mother went into town to look for lodgings. She brought back some food and milk. Tina could now swallow a little bit. The following day Mother left again with Gabi, after propping Tina up and covering her frail body with a down quilt, which came out of our suitcase. She used a white damask cover to make a real bed for little Tina and then left. I had wandered off inside the school, and when I came back, Tina was sitting up and looking much better. A young girl had given her a pair of nail scissors, and Tina was feverishly cutting out one of the repeated designs, a posy of lilies of the valley. She worked with such concentration, her large brown eyes glowing with joy again, unaware of me sitting just two feet away, admiring her skill and dexterity.

Mother returned, and Tina held out the cutout: "Look, *Mutti*, this is for you, your favorite flowers." Mother's reaction was anything but

51

joyful. Pulling the scissors out of Tina's hand, she raised her voice in anger: "This is the only decent thing we had, and you had to destroy it. Now we have nothing." Mother looked so upset; I just could not understand it. Tina had wanted to give her a beautiful present to make her happy again. She could not comprehend the reaction either; she just sat there, and slowly the sparkle in her eyes went out, her gaze went distant, and her face turned pale again.

It is strange how vividly I remember this episode, the large bare schoolroom, the dirty light-green walls, the opaque windows, and above all the smell of dust, sweat, and despair. I had inherited my mother's acute sense of smell, and even as an adult, I find that smells often invoke and trigger memories. That sense of despair mixed with bodily smells I experienced in my fifties when I took a group of adolescents to a federal high-security prison brought back the schoolroom in Gera in 1945, as if I was there again.

I can still see my beloved Tina lying there, so desolate and forlorn. She never came back to us again, at least not all of her. She had been half dead in spirit and body, and the cutout gift was the last flicker before her light seemed to go out. She was nearly seven years old and never recovered completely. She carried life as something she had not asked for. As an adolescent and young adult she would often tell me that she had not chosen to be born but that she would make sure she had a say in how and when she would exit her life.

I do not blame my mother. She must have been close to a complete breakdown. But the tragedy of that time in the schoolroom lingers in my mind and made me want to reach out to the victims of war and violence when they have appeared on the blurred screen night after night, from Vietnam, Cambodia, and the former Yugoslavia, to the many countries on the African continent, Afghanistan, Iraq, and Lebanon, to name just some. There are so many places in the world where people have to bear the unbearable; children are torn out of childhood, orphaned, and trained as soldiers to continue the senseless suffering and loss. Will we ever learn?

CHAPTER 7

We have the ability, always,
To rise above our personal lives,
To help others;
This is particularly true
During natural and man-made disasters.
—Sabina de Werth Neu

We stayed in the school for a few more days. Mother went out daily scrounging for food and looking for a place for us to live. We were now in the Soviet part of the former Germany, and as Tina was still very weak, there was no easy way to go farther west. Anyway, where were we supposed to go?

One night, Mother came back very excited. She had met an elderly couple, Ida and Richard Rothe. "They have a little grocery store, mostly with empty shelves, but they are willing to let us have a space in their attic and the use of their kitchen," she told us breathlessly. So we moved the next day, with our sparse belongings, just one suitcase now, our backpacks, and Tina riding piggyback on Herr Rothe, who led the way. Mother told us it was a miracle to have found a space, considering large sections of Gera had been destroyed by aerial bombings. In our "bedroom" under the rafters and roof tiles were two dusty old mattresses on wooden boards, but Mother fixed it up as nice as she could.

The first night we discovered that we had company. A whole family of rats ran across us at night, squeaking loudly. We crept under the covers in fear. A few nights later, a rat ran onto my face and bit me on the nose and then on my left arm. It startled me, and I shrieked. Mother turned on the bare overhead lightbulb and, after seeing the bit of blood on me, she became quite frantic, fearing we would all get the bubonic plague. We were scared, and I don't think Mother slept much at night from then on; she preferred to watch over her three precious girls. Keeping us alive, safe, fed, and clean were the main reasons for her to keep going.

Our diet consisted mostly of potatoes and, a few times, just potato peelings, which Mother washed carefully and boiled to make a lumpy paste. It did not taste too bad, especially with substitute jam, a red jellylike spread sweetened with saccharin. Sometimes we had some real bread and a little skimmed milk. The Rothes shared what little they had, sometimes a carrot or turnip or something really exotic, like a cucumber or some early sour apples.

As the weeks went on, Mother could hardly go outside. She would lie lifeless and pale on the bug-infested mattress. We sat close to her, not daring to make a sound, sweating under the roof beams in the dimly lit room. There was a tiny, cracked, dirty window at the far end of the attic, but there was little or no ventilation. Gabi eventually went downstairs to get Frau Rothe, who arranged to get us all to a nearby hospital. Mother could hardly stand up and had to lean on Herr Rothe to get downstairs to a waiting truck.

It turned out that Mother was seriously ill, so the doctor kept her in the hospital. After examining us girls, he sent us to the basement ward, where the sick children were kept; only women were allowed upstairs. The separation from our mother was terrible for us. We had been through so much and now felt utterly abandoned. I remember nearly burning up from crying so much. But at least we were now getting food three times a day—thin whole-wheat noodle soup, bread, milk, honey, and some fruit, mainly apples, plums, and pears.

After a few days we were allowed to visit *Mutti* upstairs. She looked thin and small, like a complete stranger in the big metal bed. I remember feeling like a caged, frightened bird, eager to see the outside world. Before anyone could stop me I had climbed onto the windowsill of the second-story open window to see the sky and some trees. Mother shrieked and someone grabbed me from behind. Then she sobbed so pitifully, having already imagined me landing on the hard asphalt below. I felt so guilty and sure that it was my fault she was ill and that now she would probably die because of me.

Only many years later did I find out that my mother had gonorrhea and a very messy miscarriage, a result of the gang rape by the Russian soldiers. The three of us were also treated for venereal disease, just in case. In the absence of antibiotics, the only treatment in those days was some kind of sulfur injection, which had to be administered several times per week for a complete year, straight into our small skinny behinds. There is not enough room on a small child's buttocks to receive around 150 injections. We became human pincushions. After our release from the hospital, I dreaded each visit there, and the fear of needles has stayed with me to this day. The only needles I now take willingly are those from my Chinese acupuncturist.

When we got back to our cramped quarters with the Rothe family, we found out that Ida Rothe's sisters and nephews, also refugees, needed our space. Since Mother was now much better, she went hunting for a job, as we had to find new accommodations. Around the corner, Mother found work and lodgings all in one. The owner of a rather seedy restaurant and bar gave us two upstairs rooms with an electric hot plate and a separate toilet with washbasin. In exchange my mother had to mop the bathrooms, hallways, and staircase twice a day, but she got a small amount of money if she did it well. This situation was better than we could have expected, and it gave Mother enough time to get another job at a tailor where she was mostly mending clothes.

Now things were looking up. Mother brought home apples and cabbages, bread, milk, and a few luxury items like a small jar of honey, berries from the woods, and sometimes an unidentifiable piece of meat. Mostly it was horsemeat, or so we assumed, but we tried not to think about the possibilities. Mother also procured woolen fabric to make winter clothes for us all. The tailor allowed her to use one of his sewing machines.

A LONG SILENCE

On one of our many visits to the hospital—using the tram because it was raining—Tina jumped off before the tram stopped. Mother's emotional reaction seemed so exaggerated to me; I did not understand how frayed her nerves must have been. She could not calm down for the longest time, whereas I admired Tina's ability and courage to jump without falling. She had looked more like a young deer than a child as she was flying into the air.

The memories of my two sisters, especially Gabi, are quite hazy and intermittent. Like most children, I lived in my own universe, with my own perceptions and emotions. But I do recall the spring of 1946, when my sisters both went off on a "youth excursion" to some kind of sanatorium in the forest of Thuringia, in a place called *Finsterbergen*, meaning, literally, "gloomy mountains." I was glad I did not have to go. It sounded like a witch's place from *Hansel and Gretel*. And I could go to work with my mother and felt very special as an only child for a little while.

CHAPTER 8

Schliesse mir die Augen beide
Mit den lieben Händen zu!
Geht doch alles was ich leide,
Unter deiner Hand zur Ruh.

Close both my eyes
with your dear hands!
Under your hand
All my sufferings are assuaged.
—Theodor Storm (1817–1888), "Close Both My Eyes"

During my sisters' time at the sanatorium, when I was about four and a half years old, I became sick with an earache, a sore throat, a terrible cough, and a high fever. A nurse was called, and in no time at all I was torn from my mother's arms, struggling and crying, and put into a waiting ambulance outside. I sat on a narrow seat, very close to a strange woman lying on a stretcher. She was covered in blood, and her skin was the color of a dirty towel. I just knew she was dead, like old Farmer Friedel, and I was terrified that the ambulance driver was going to take us somewhere to be buried together.

The ambulance suddenly stopped, the back doors opened, and two men pulled the stretcher out. I was holding my breath, expecting the worst. But we moved again, turning many corners, and then I realized we were leaving town. I was so relieved, but I peeped out below the frosted glass of the back window to see where we were going. I saw mostly trees, and somehow this comforted me.

A LONG SILENCE

Finally we stopped, the door opened, and someone lifted me out. Everywhere I looked there were long wooden barracks. Before I could take it all in, a nurse came toward me, picked me up, and brought me to a doctor in one of the huts. Everyone was very nice and explained to me where I was. It was a place for children with infectious diseases, a kind of quarantine hospital. I was here for suspected diphtheria and scarlet fever. My skin was all blotchy, and I was burning from deep inside. My ears hurt so much that I had to bite my lower lip, because I did not want to be a crybaby.

I awoke in a long room with many beds, bad smells, and the sound of other children crying and moaning. My bed was next to a window, which was partially open. I could see and hear the tops of large spruce trees moving and sighing in the wind. The cooling breeze caressed my hot face and hands. I drifted off to sleep again. When I opened my eyes I was so confused. How far away from Gera was I? I was certain that I would never see my mother and sisters again. This was where I would have to live for the rest of my life.

I was in this place for many weeks—to me it seemed like months— but I was slowly getting better and gaining strength. The best thing was that I was no longer hungry. It was a very wonderful feeling. I got food several times a day—dark noodle soup, cabbage and other vegetables I didn't know, bread and milk with real jam, rice pudding with dried fruit, and occasionally a piece of sweet hard caramel wrapped in brown paper.

I was getting used to this new life, especially falling asleep to the whispering of the trees, the isolation from the world, the new feeling of being secure, and the kindness of the nurses. There were no men around in my new world; the doctors in their white coats did not really count. The nurses reminded me of our Hertha back in East Prussia, kind and always smiling. I was able to walk around in my hospital gown, down the long corridor of our barrack. Sometimes one of the nurses stroked my blonde curls, and I felt happy for a short while.

One sunny day, I was packed into the ambulance with several other children. We were going home. This time it was not frightening. After a long ride we could see houses and even a few cars and people on bicycles. One by one the children were dropped off. Then it was my turn, and finally I stood in front of the restaurant and bar where we lived, wearing the same clothes I wore when I was taken away. Since it was the middle of the morning, the doors were still closed. I sat down on the sidewalk, leaning against the dirty building, not really expecting anyone to come.

But suddenly I saw a familiar figure running around the corner. It was my sister Tina, calling out my name, over and over again. Then Mother and Gabi emerged around the corner. I must have been in some kind of shock, because my legs would not move and I could not get up. Mother scooped me up, and I took in her wonderful smell. Then I started to cry all the tears that I had stored up inside my heart for all this long, long time.

CHAPTER 9

Ich zieh in Krieg auf grüne Heid;
Die grüne Heid, sie ist so weit!
Allwo dort die schönen Trompeten blasen,
Da ist mein Haus von grünem Rasen.

I go to war in green fields,
the green fields stretch so far!
Where the splendid trumpets blow
there is my home of green turf.
—from "Des Knaben Wunderhorn," German folk poems,
reworked by Achim von Arnim and Clemens Brentano,
nineteenth century

Things had gotten much better while I had been away. There was more food and finally some pillows and clean, softer blankets. We got skimmed milk every day, and Mother made *Muckefuk*, a brown liquid made with boiling water and ground roasted acorns—a coffee substitute, at least in color. When sweetened with saccharin and added milk it was very satisfying and helped to keep us warm during the wet spring mornings. We dipped our bread in it and had a delicious breakfast. I often think of it when staying in a fancy hotel and coming down for a nearly sinful breakfast buffet. How did I get from there to here, I ask myself at such a moment?

Mother had been writing many letters to her family and had found out that our grandmother and Aunt Marga had survived the war in Görlitz, Silesia, the town where Gabi was born in 1935. In late spring of

Sabina in the meadow, Gera, Thuringia, East Germany

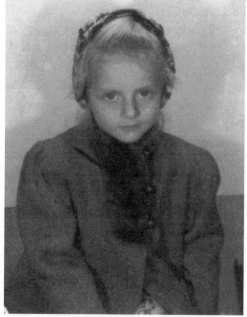

Sabina, identification photo, Gera, 1946

1946 we went to the local railway station to await their visit. It was a bittersweet reunion. *Omi* (Grandma) had received a letter from the *Wehrmacht* (army) in November of 1944 that her beloved son Kurt, our *Onkel* Kurt, had gone missing in action on October 6 of that year in a fierce battle with the Red Army at Kalnujai, four miles south of Raseinen, Lithuania (maybe in green fields where splendid trumpets blew). The letter said it was possible that Officer Kurt Maskus had been taken prisoner by the Russians. We were all sad. Mother cried a lot and was convinced that her brother was dead.

Despite the news about *Onkel* Kurt, I felt good to have more family; we were stronger now, with three adults and three children. I tried to console *Omi* by sitting on her lap and letting her talk about her Kurt. She was sure he was still alive and would soon be released. She clung to this hope for the next twenty-four years, until her death in 1968. *Tante* Marga had tried to contact our relatives, who had lived mostly in Dresden and Breslau, Silesia. All the letters came back marked "address no longer exists, street leveled by bombs." So any uncles, aunts, and cousins we had, had vanished forever.

During the visit, we did a lot of walking, especially during the main part of the day, when Gabi and Tina were at school. Walking and hiking had been a tradition with my grandparents, and I soon learned to march on my skinny legs right alongside the adults. On one of these walks on the outskirts of town I felt particularly energetic and confident. I ran ahead, off the path and under a group of trees, where I found myself in a large uncut meadow.

The long grasses were taller than I was and moved sideways as I passed, like sentinels, then closed their ranks again. I stopped and looked at this new world. Everything smelled so good. I heard the rasping of the crickets, the hum of countless insects; it sounded like a very delicate kind of music. The colors of the flowers were mostly blue and yellow, pink and white, and bees sat in their centers, pushing their heads deep inside as if planting kisses. I lay down on my back, looking up at the blue sky and the white downy clouds moving across. Butter-

Sabina and Mother, *"nach all dem Elend"*

Sabina, Mother, *Omi*, and friend, Gera

flies in many colors and patterns undulated just above me. Birdsong came across from a distance. I lay quite still and was overcome by a feeling of utter peace and well-being. I must have entered heaven at last, and now all the misery of my little life was gone.

But then I heard my name being called over and over, by *Mutti* first, then by *Omi* and *Tante* Marga. I got up and ran back to them, and the magic was over.

Throughout my life, I continue to return to this place—in my mind—whenever I feel the need, to fill myself with wonder and a sense that all is right with the world. At the age of nearly five, this experience was the first and crucial step in my healing. Since then the natural world has become a nourishing source from which I can drink when I am thirsty, even today.

The thought of food continued to be ever present in my mind. On a walk in town with Mother and *Tante* Marga, I stopped in front of a small shop window, which had as its only display a glass bowl filled with water and one lone goldfish swimming in circles. Salivating, I exclaimed: "Oh, I want him fried!" When the two adult sisters burst out laughing, I corrected myself, thinking I had made a culinary mistake, by saying "Or steamed!" which produced even more laughter. I never lived this incident down. In my defense I must mention how hungry we all were for a bit of protein, no matter how small.

Mother took us to a photographer's studio to have passport photos made for identification papers. There is a photograph with Mother and me, and Mother is smiling, as am I. On the back of the photo, in Mother's angular handwriting, I found "*nach all dem Elend,* 1946" ("after all the misery, 1946"). Maybe she, too, felt that the worst suffering had now come to an end.

CHAPTER 10

Und morgen wird die Sonne wieder scheinen
Und auf dem Wege, den ich gehen werde,
Wird uns, die Glücklichen, sie wieder einen
Inmitten dieser sonnenatmenden Erde . . .

And tomorrow the sun will shine again
and on the path we walk in our happiness
it will again unite us
in the midst of this sun-drenched earth . . .
　　　　　—John Henry Mackay (1864–1933), from "Morgen,"
　　　　　　set to music by Richard Strauss (1894)

In the autumn of 1946 we were on the move again. *Omi* and *Tante* Marga had returned to Görlitz, and Mother had obtained tickets for a train to Eisenach. Her intention was to get out of the Soviet-occupied part of Germany, the part that was becoming Communist East Germany; she hoped to reach the southern part of Germany, which was under American occupation. Mother's fear of the Russians lasted nearly her entire life. At the time I did not know nor could I have understood how brutally she had been raped by scores of soldiers and how many unspeakable brutalities against women she witnessed afterward, in the weeks when we waited for a train in Zwittau. Women were tied to the backs of two army trucks, which then drove at high speed in opposite directions, tearing them in half while still alive. And there was more that Mother could not bring herself to utter. Only once did she talk to me about that time in short staccato sentences, when I was about twenty and she was fifty years old. After that, nothing more was ever mentioned again, just as if it never happened. How on earth did she survive what today would be described as post-traumatic stress disorder?

Today I look at history and the war on women and children in particular and realize that it has been going on for centuries. Victimizing women and children in times of war seems to be the ultimate act of rage and revenge by men against the enemy they are fighting. It is an expression of their own victimization that has made them into legalized killers, outside of good and evil.

We boarded the train to Eisenach and beyond, and before long the train came to a slow stop near a sign announcing Gerstingen. It was very dark outside, no moon or stars, as we piled out of the train, thousands of us. You could hear some whispering, but it was eerily quiet. We moved in the dark in a long endless line, stepping lightly, afraid to make any sound. I was carrying my little rucksack again with the small chamber pot tied on the back. Mother had no hands for us, stooping under an enormous bundle on her back and having to change the heavy suitcase from side to side. We girls followed like goslings behind the mother goose. The ground beneath us smelled of mushrooms and wet leaves, changing to pine needles every now and then. The trek seemed without end and often turned rocky. My feet and legs were hurting, and often I had to run in order to keep up, as someone in the front had set the pace, fast and determined, and we had no choice but to follow.

We were refugees, fugitives, hoping to find some kind of safe haven ahead, but mainly we were fleeing from something, escaping, running away. We had joined the millions of other dispossessed, desperate, and homeless.

There was a border to cross, a new train waiting on the other side, and another occupation of soldiers to endure. But I trusted Mother's intuition that life would be better under the American forces. In late morning we crossed a railway line and saw a stationary train waiting some distance away. Before we boarded, strange-looking men and women in dark blue uniforms, clean and smiling, gave us tea, milk, and big chunks of white bread. Who were they? Their hats and armbands showed a red cross. Once on the train, Mother told us about the wonderful people of the American Red Cross. We settled down in the clean train—even the toilets were usable—and we felt better despite the long night's march. I slept until we reached Bebra, a huge railway junction, where everybody had to get off.

Buses and trucks took us to a large refugee camp. There we had to wait for several weeks in huge army tents while our papers were being processed, waiting in long lines in cold and wet weather. We were devoured by bed bugs and had to be treated for head lice. Now we really looked like the scum of humanity, the refuse of war. Mother suffered in all the dirt and ugliness, about which she could do little.

One day a lady from the Red Cross came to see us in our corner with good news. They had located my father in southern Germany in the city of Stuttgart and notified him. Mother cried with relief.

Locating people was relatively easy, even without computers, as all citizens had to register with the local authorities and supply the place of domicile in order to get an identity card. The victors of World War II had not dismantled the government departments and the German efficiency was still very much in evidence.

Soon it was time to leave the camp for the Bebra railway station with four one-way tickets to Stuttgart. The station was teeming with refugees as Mother frantically tried to find the platform where our train would arrive. We raced down the dirty concrete steps that went under the rails, then up the next steps, but it was the wrong platform. Down again we went, under and up, pushing through throngs of people with baggage. At the top of yet another flight of steps, I got separated from my mother and sisters; people were pushing me this way and that, and I had trouble staying on my feet. I started to cry out, but nobody heard me; I could only see trouser legs and felt rough woolen coats scratching my face.

Eventually I found myself in the tunnel under the rails and pressed myself against the wall so as not to be swept away any farther. I felt nauseated with panic and was awash with tears. After an eternity a woman noticed me, grabbed me firmly by the hand, and took me to the office of the *Bahnpolizei* (railroad station police). There Mother finally claimed me. She was sweating and out of sorts and did not understand why I could not have held on any tighter. I went on sobbing for a long time, still feeling abandoned, despite having been found.

In the end we managed to board the right train and after many stops and pauses finally arrived at Stuttgart *Hauptbahnhof* (main station). There my father, whom I barely remembered, picked us out among all the other bedraggled arrivals.

CHAPTER 11

**Get up, I depend
on you utterly.
Everything you need
you had
the moment before
you were born.**

—David Whyte (1955–),
"Waking," from *Where Many Rivers Meet* (1990)

My sister Gabi, who was then eleven years old, remembers our father welcoming us with open arms. I find that difficult to believe, considering what happened later that day. But children's memories are by their very nature highly subjective. Gabi at her prepubescent age was longing for a father figure. She had had a strong bond with Father and clear memories of him from before the war, and she continued to be his favorite daughter right up to his death in 1963.

Perhaps because of my young age and the circumstances, he didn't make much of an impression on me. In fact, my memory of that morning in October 1946 is less of him than of a bronze statue of a naked boy, which fascinated me. It stood in the middle of a fountain in a circle of row houses, and from his penis flowed a magnificently curved stream of water into the large basin of the fountain.

The house where Father brought us was the property of a rotund woman named Johanna Simon, a war widow with whom Father had been living. He was doing more than just occupying a space in her house: he was also sleeping in her bed and wearing her dead husband's suits since the end of the war. I am sure the poor woman had hoped we would never show up, and I have a suspicion that Father had given up on us and thought he was sitting pretty.

For my mother, the situation must have been the last straw. She was speechless and close to tears as we climbed the stairs to yet another attic to make a mattress camp under the rafters, while my father continued to share the widow's conjugal bed. I did not like this woman, Johanna, because she caused Mother such terrible pain. Her red fingernails looked evil to me, and I could hardly bear to look at her.

I can now, as an adult, understand how Mother must have felt. After all the horrors, terrors, hunger, and misery, she must have longed so much to be reunited with her husband, the father of her three girls, whom she had saved so courageously. She had held it together, barely, hoping he would now take over and she could lean on him and rest a bit and be comforted. Instead she found him with another woman. (I discovered later that having affairs had been a habit of his even before I was conceived.) But the letdown must have been devastating for her just the same.

A few days after our arrival in Stuttgart, Mother broke apart. The three of us were outside on a brisk, sunny October morning, playing catch. Mother had slept so soundly that morning that we had gotten up quietly by ourselves, so as not to wake her. Around noon an ambulance drove into the square and stopped in front of Frau Simon's house. Two men went inside with a stretcher and emerged almost instantly. I could see that my mother's face was as gray as the blanket that covered the rest of her. She looked dead. I could not move. I just stood there as if frozen to the spot and followed the ambulance with my eyes until it disappeared around the corner.

A leaden heaviness and a feeling of abandonment enveloped me, more terrible than anything that had gone before. Within my five-year-old heart I knew that my father had done this, had taken her from us, because he had no love to give her, only pain. From that moment on I started to hate him.

I poured all the love I still had left onto my sister Tina, who was in worse shape than me. Gabi meanwhile spent time with Johanna and our father—her father, really, and I did not like her for doing it.

Mother eventually returned to us from the hospital. She had taken an overdose of sleeping tablets, which she must have hoarded for years. Her eyes sat deep in her face, the dark circles underneath accentuating them. Her cheekbones were so sharp they appeared about to push through her fine skin. She had to see a special doctor once a week, and I no longer dared to hope that she would return every time she left the house.

The long and cold winter of 1946–47 is like a blur now. In order to survive I tried to banish the feelings of despair, the shame of being a refugee, the shame of having had such terrible things happen to my body. But it was to no avail.

Living in an attic again, homeless and unwanted, I only remember a gnawing feeling of hopelessness and fear, believing that life would continue like this forever.

Like most child victims of abuse, I tried to make sense of my experience with my limited mental reasoning. I must have somehow deserved all the punishment and suffering, because I was innately bad. There was a certain survival-based logic in this. If true, then I could change my destiny. By being extra good, I could have control over what happened to me in the future.

That determination and belief stayed with me for a long time. I embraced the Roman Catholic faith with hope, only to discover that I was unable to live up to all the saintly behavior, which only added to my fears and anxieties of more punishments and suffering, not just in this life, but beyond. I really tried hard to be good but failed again and again.

That winter, Tina and I spent a lot of time wrapped in blankets next to my mother, stroking and combing her wavy brown hair. Every now and then there would be a few milder days, and we would take walks along a small stream nearby—the Ramsbach—which also carried raw sewage; steam would rise from it in the cold winter air. By March we could pick the first pussy willows and later the first purple violets, which had a wonderful scent and remained one of Mother's favorite flowers.

A LONG SILENCE

Looking back now, it must have been very hard for Johanna Simon, who, after all, cooked and washed for us. She must have hoped that her beloved Bernd, my father, would get a separation and that she would eventually marry the then forty-two-year-old man. She had befriended him after he was released from a British prisoner-of-war camp, where he had helped the Brits as a clerk. He was extremely handsome and related well to women, a sort of mixture of the French actor and singer Maurice Chevalier and the debonair British thespian George Sanders. His light-blue eyes had a soulful expression, and few women could resist him. Even some of Mother's female friends would succumb to his charms over time (and there were also hints that her own sister was among his intimates).

In the spring of 1947, the resettlement authorities allocated two rooms for us in a beautiful villa in the suburb of Degerloch, nearby. Owners of big houses had to give up rooms to help house the thousands of refugees. Mother revived at the thought of getting out of our current situation. She loved the street names of our new corner-house address: on one side was Waldstrasse (Forest Street) and on the other side Silberpappelweg (Silver Poplar Lane).

Our new landlords were called Neuwirth, meaning "new landlord" in German, which Mother saw as a good omen. The Neuwirths had two teenage sons and had to move upstairs, but they kept the kitchen and elegant foyer on the first floor. We got one decent-sized room over the double garage, overlooking the paved driveway. The other room was an enormous space with a sculptured fireplace, huge windows, and French doors, which opened onto a flagstone terrace shaded by a pergola with wisteria vines growing in profusion, creating a dreamlike canopy for us. I had never seen anything so beautiful.

Mother paced out the large space and announced that it was eleven meters, thirty centimeters long (about thirty-four feet), and called it our *Sälchen* (little ballroom). The shiny parquet floor was inlaid in different colored woods. Later, one of our hardest chores was to keep it waxed and polished, all on our knees. We used the French doors as our front door, so as not to interfere with our landlords. The only time we could cross the marble-tiled foyer was to use the tiny guest bathroom downstairs, which had a toilet and a very small sink with running cold water. This is where we washed ourselves and rinsed our mouths at bedtime.

Father had come with us when we moved. Maybe he was not enough of a scoundrel to abandon us completely at that time, at least not that abruptly, seeing how fragile Mother was. Instead, his abandonment was stretched out over years, a kind of prolonged torture for his suffering wife. But he did try to provide for us. He went out daily looking for work and acquiring secondhand furniture from the Red Cross and other charities, and bartering for all sorts of household necessities. Mother had a real knack for transforming beat-up objects with paint or covering them with fabric, and she used space in a most creative way. So our space soon felt like a real home, and she seemed more at peace with all the activity.

During the summer we lived and ate mostly outside on the wonderful terrace, looking out on a beautiful flower garden and lilac hedge. Mother had dyed some sheets vermillion red and hung them from the ceiling of the *Sälchen* to create space for a sleeping area, where there were two single beds for Father and her along one wall and window. In the summer, the three-tiered bunk beds (I, being the lightest, was always on top) were moved from the opposite wall to the small room above the garage, which during the winter had contained our living room furniture, table, chairs, and an old sofa next to the only stove. As we did not have the heat on anymore, this furniture was now spread out in the remaining space of the ballroom.

I loved this seasonal moving around; our living area seemed a new place each time. But our landlord can't have been thrilled hearing the furniture being dragged across his precious parquet floor. We tried to repolish the inevitable scratches that occurred, but it did not always work.

Two large old armoires at the sleeping end of the *Sälchen* created a partition for the last six feet, where we made a makeshift counter and shelves with bricks and long old boards. Here Mother prepared our meals and stored what food and pots we had.

In the very left-hand corner was a door to a landing for the steep steps that led down to the cellar. The landing had a small enamel sink and a small gas stove, just two burners, no oven. This was our kitchen proper.

Every Saturday afternoon, while my sisters went to confession at our Catholic church, I would follow Mother down into the cellar where she would light an old, coal-burning hot-water boiler to get ready for our once-a-week bath time. She had to fill the boiler with water from a rubber hose, and in a few hours there would be enough hot water to fill the large zinc bathtub, which hung on the wall. I could help her to get it down and slide it into position on the cold concrete floor, close to a drain, where she would fill bucket after bucket with steaming hot water and adjust the temperature by adding cold water from the hose.

There was a strict hierarchy as to who would go first: Gabi, being the firstborn, would get sparkling clear water to sit in; Tina was next; and by the time it was my turn, the water was cloudy and soapy. But I did not mind, as Mother would add extra hot water, and I could sit in the sisterly soup quite a long time, until it was time to have my hair rinsed with clear water ladled from a bucket. I can still feel the roughness of the towel Mother wrapped around me as I finally stepped out into the now humid air of the boiler room, which also doubled as a laundry room for washday. It was the height of luxury to be dried and rubbed, to put on a clean nightie and have Mother make a turban on my head with a dishcloth to keep my hair from dripping.

In the winter months we raced upstairs, through the icy *Sälchen* into the heated living room. There it was cozy, and one could dry one's hair close to the hot coal stove, often so close that Mother would get alarmed when she smelled singed hair. I think later, when we were in bed, she and Father would tip out the bathwater and refill it for their own cleaning.

Only when I discovered later how my school friends lived, with real bathrooms, kitchens, and so on, did I realize how poor we were and how primitively we lived. I never told anyone how we kept ourselves clean. It became just another item I added to my list of things to be ashamed of and to keep hidden.

When I was lucky to be sick during the summer months, Mother would make a daybed out on the terrace. I remember spending glorious days out there when I had the chicken pox, despite the terrible itching. Above me was the wisteria sky; birds were singing; the gray schnauzer was chasing something real or imagined; and his owner, Herr Neuwirth, would peek through the leaves for a little chat. Summers were long and sunny and splendid then, time moving slowly like melting toffee on a baking sheet.

CHAPTER 12

September sunshine . . .
The hovering
Dragonfly's
Shimmering shadow.

—Karo, from *The Four Seasons:*
Japanese Haiku by Bashō Matsuo

The year 1947 was the year I started to resume my childhood, which had been interrupted by the events since we left East Prussia. Mother had enrolled me in kindergarten (more a preschool than an American kindergarten), and she allowed me to walk there all by myself, which made me feel very proud and independent. I walked all the way to the end of the Silberpappelweg and turned right along a lovely footpath at the edge of the municipal forest on one side and a vast apple orchard on the other.

The kindergarten was on the first floor of a large brick building down a hill and had two enormous sandpits in the back as well as room to run around. Most of the other children were much bigger and heavier than I was. They were mostly local children from Swabian (a region west of Bavaria) stock and spoke a strange, thick German dialect, so I had to learn to stand up for myself. It was easy to pick on me; I was skinny and spoke "real" German. My first encounter was in the sandpit with a fat boy who tried to hit me with his little metal shovel. I ducked, and before he could continue I hit him back with mine and drew some blood from his forehead. I felt terrible about what I had done, but the result was that from then on the children left me alone despite my puny size.

This was a memorable experience of really feeling different from other children, of feeling like an outcast and less than the others. My young mind was more convinced than ever that we had somehow deserved what had happened to us. This strong feeling of being different and bad and the accompanying shame would remain for a large part of my life, despite my attempts to excel and to delight others. The truth was that I had no belief in myself, and no amount of praise and recognition could change that. I did everything I could not to act, look, or behave like a victim, scum, or dirty refugee. I learned to live on the surface of things, trying to hide my wounded heart even from myself, but I was not always successful.

The most vivid memory I have of going to kindergarten was the walk home one very sultry summer's day. Dark clouds were racing over the swaying treetops, as the wind kicked up, swirling the dust from the ground and lifting my dress. Soon the flash and boom of lightning and thunder came in quick succession, and then enormous, heavy raindrops began to fall on me. I was not afraid of the thunderstorm, but I was worried about what damage the storm might do to my clothes and shoes. So I stopped under a large oak tree, took everything off except my underpants, rolled it all into a tight bundle, shoes in the middle, and walked home through mud and deep puddles. Down Silberpappelweg I marched, through *Donner* and *Blitzen* (thunder and lightning), as water poured over my head and face, and my sorry little underpants barely clung to my small behind.

Oh, the fuss Mother made when I came through the terrace doors! She wrapped me in all available towels, talked of pneumonia, death by lightning, and other dire consequences. I, on the other hand, was full of myself and pleased to have kept my shoes out of the rain. Shoes were hard to come by and not too sturdy back then. The inner soles were made of cardboard, and the glue that held the outer sole to the body of the shoe could easily separate. Despite my mother's reaction, I had found this wild weather rather exhilarating. Through much of my life I have run out naked into downpours whenever privacy allowed such childish behavior. I have always trusted nature, believing it is other humans one has to be wary of.

In September 1947, Mother took me to the local elementary school to enroll me in first grade. I was just three weeks shy of my sixth birthday and very eager and excited. Both my sisters could read and write, and I did not want to be left behind. I was inspected and poked around by a fat, bald man who wore a monocle. After asking my mother many questions, he pulled down the corners of his mouth, shook his head from side to side, and said to my mother: "That will never do. She is far too thin and small. Bring her back next September."

Oh, the disappointment and humiliation! I felt rejected and did not understand what thin or fat had to do with writing, reading, or arithmetic. After all, I was not a pig being inspected for going to market. Today I suspect that this doctor might have seen more than my skinny little body. Maybe he could see the frightened little girl with inner scars who needed more healing before being thrown into a classroom of forty kids, most of them locals.

Mother, I thought, was quite glad to have me home for another year. She had not made any new friends, and I was good company. So we spent wonderful mornings foraging for wild food in the forest. We picked many pounds of ripe, shiny blackberries, and I got used to getting my hands scratched by the thorns. We'd gather wild sorrel, elderberries, and, most of all, mushrooms and wild fungi. Mother possessed a squirrel's instinct and feverishly prepared for the approaching winter. We hunted, literally, for mushrooms, outsmarting and outguessing the many people who did the same. Mother had gotten an excellent education from her father, who had been an expert mycologist. She could identify nearly all the edible species and knew which ones to leave alone.

One day we were deep in the forest, off any paths, and Mother, following her marvelous sense of smell, homed in on a large rotten tree trunk on the ground. It was covered with hundreds, maybe thousands, of light-brown umbrella-shaped fungi. Mother was beside herself with joy. We picked enough to fill both our sacks, but there was no way to carry them all home. So we stole back, marking our trail by bending over some branches, to find the spot again.

The next morning before daybreak, Mother borrowed Herr

Neuwirth's wooden cart, a rack wagon, and several empty burlap sacks. Three hours later she was back, sweaty and elated: "This will get us through the winter; mushrooms are like meat." The remainder of that day and the next, with my sisters' help after school, we cleaned and strung up hundreds upon hundreds of "'rooms," hanging them up above the terrace from the wires of the pergola. The name of our miraculous crop was *Hallimasche* (a fungus of the honey mushroom, also known as *Armillaria*). We children eventually got tired of them and were glad when we finished the last of them before Easter the following year.

I spent much time in Herr Neuwirth's garden. He often came home before dark, as gardening and looking after his chickens was one of his favorite things to do. He was so patient with me, answering my endless questions about everything that came into my head. Sometimes, when his wife was out, he gave us some fresh eggs. I still remember my first soft-boiled egg. It was indescribably wonderful, and I ate it very slowly, eyes closed, making the experience more intense.

Frau Neuwirth was less friendly, but who could blame her? She had to give up so much of her beautiful home for us. We had to be very quiet when playing, and if something displeased her, she would complain and threaten Mother with eviction. This caused her to be in a constant state of anxiety.

I can't recall my father being home very much. He was trying many different jobs and "had many irons in the fire," as Mother explained. I did not understand what that meant. We only had one iron, so why did he need many, especially as I had never seen him iron anything?

Often he stayed out all night. This would put Mother in a decline, and she would stay in bed weeping quietly. It became my job to cheer her up by making cups of chamomile or peppermint tea from the crops we had gathered during the summer. I sweetened it with saccharin; sugar was too precious, as we got only 100 grams (three and a half ounces) a month with our ration cards. Often I would bring her back late-autumn flowers from the roadside or brightly colored leaves, which didn't last but glowed for a few hours. She would say: "Oh, my little

Binchen" (her affectionate nickname for me), "What has become of me?" and turn her face to the wall, sobbing. I felt so terribly helpless.

I think after a few months Father got a job as a buyer for men's clothes at Union, one of the remaining department stores in downtown Stuttgart. Most of the center had been heavily bombed in the last years of the war, including the beautiful castle (in the style of Versailles) of the king of Württemberg. To me it all looked pretty normal, the ruins of buildings and rubble everywhere. I had never seen a city in peacetime.

Father worked long hours and traveled quite a bit, while Mother grew more and more uneasy, as she could not trust him. Because of the war, there was a shortage of men, and thus there were many widows, young adult women and orphans, as well an endless array of traumatized women who were hungry for a man of my father's qualities: his sympathy, charm, and understanding, no matter how superficial. They swarmed toward him like moths to a candle. Some of these descriptions came out of my mother's mouth; she was jealous beyond reason.

For my father it must have been heady stuff, and he did not have the moral strength to resist. However, he appeared to like the idea of having a beautiful wife at home who needed him and, I believe, loved him. Being married also helped him, as he didn't have to make any commitments.

There were constant fights and accusations, followed by short reconciliations with much sentimentality on my father's side. Then all of a sudden we played happy family again. I sort of got used to these ups and downs. I think the reason I was not more damaged was that I had few expectations in regards to *Vati* (Daddy). He was a background figure, made of cardboard, and sent to make my mother immensely unhappy. What it left in me, however, was a big void, a ravenous "father hunger," which would lead me, in later years, into the company of older men and into more trouble and suffering.

There was, however, a time in the fall of 1947, when I felt, for some afternoons, that we were a real family. Father came home early with two heavy suitcases. One was filled with aluminum screwdrivers, the other with adjustable roller skates made of the same metal. The idea was to take the tram to the limits of Degerloch and from there walk from farm to farm and barter the merchandise for food. Tina felt ashamed and said, "I do not want to be a beggar." But I was happy at the prospect of getting more food and walking in the countryside, seeing animals, smelling dung heaps, looking at beetles and spiders, and stroking barnyard cats.

One farmer's wife gave Tina and me each a huge red-cheeked apple, the size of a newborn baby's head. I needed both my hands to hold it. The apple was sweet and sour at the same time, and the juice ran down over my chin and arms, dripping from my pointed elbows onto my skirt. It took me all afternoon to devour it. I have never forgotten this apple and have looked for one like it during many autumns of my life.

The screwdrivers were totally useless, as they would bend if too much pressure was applied to them. The roller skates were no better; they could break in half when one hit a bump and send the rider flying. The farms had mainly dirt roads leading to them, so the only motivation for the farmer or his wife to exchange the flawed contraptions for apples, vegetables, flour, or a rare piece of salty bacon was their generosity of heart, maybe mixed with a slight sense of guilt that they were relatively well off and well fed compared to us. Mother attributed our success to my charm and openness, as well as my blonde curls and blue eyes. What I remember the most is the adventure of those few trips, the wild purple asters along the roadside, finding fresh mushrooms under trees, and the warm autumn sun on our backs.

To this day I get this sense of adventure and acute pleasure, especially when traveling abroad in a less-developed country. In the 1990s, I had the opportunity to walk through rural areas of China and Vietnam. That trip was strangely reminiscent of the immediate postwar years around Stuttgart.

CHAPTER 13

O beautiful for patriot dream
That sees beyond the years
Thine alabaster cities gleam
Undimmed by human tears!
America! America!
God shed his grace on thee
And crown thy good with brotherhood
From sea to shining sea!
—Katharine Lee Bates, "America the Beautiful" (1913)

In September 1948, at nearly seven years old, I was finally accepted into first grade. On the first day of school, forty young girls were packed into a schoolroom; the boys were across the hallway. We were handed a wooden-framed slate with a hole in one corner from which two pieces of string held a slate pencil and a little brown natural sponge. I was more excited than frightened to finally be able to learn to write. The slate had etched horizontal lines on one side, and we immediately started to copy the big white strokes the teacher put on the blackboard with a large piece of chalk that squeaked. There was no orientation, and as far as I remember, we went straight to business. I held the pencil too tightly, causing it to break frequently. This is when I realized that writing would not be as easy as I had thought. Later, learning the alphabet and reading were much more fun, as was arithmetic.

Religious instruction, however, made me very uneasy, as I found out that I fell short of the expected standards. With my many small transgressions, I was certainly destined for hell rather than heaven.

Sabina, school photo

Going to school at last, 1948

On the third day, school really started. We had to be there from eight in the morning to noon and either go home for lunch or stay at school until afternoon classes resumed at one thirty, finishing about three. My walk to school took me nearly thirty minutes, so I usually stayed at school.

During my first lunchtime we all had to gather in single file outside in the asphalt schoolyard. Two khaki-green army trucks were parked at the metal gates. Several extremely tall, smiling soldiers were handing out small aluminum canteens with lids, spoons, and forks along the side. These soldiers had no guns or helmets, and they looked so clean, well fed, and friendly. I had never seen uniformed men look that way and was not scared at all. The girl behind me explained that they were *Amis* (short for *Amerikaners*). In retrospect, what a fitting abbreviation, as *amis* means "friends" in French, and these men turned out to be our friends indeed.

The line moved slowly toward the open trucks. When it was my turn, I could smell something so good that my mouth filled with saliva. A black-skinned soldier with sparkling white teeth took my canteen, reached up into a square metal container, and returned the steaming canteen to me, filled to the brim. I nodded in thanks and curtsied, which made him smile even more.

For the next fifteen minutes all my senses were directed toward the contents of my little pot. I still remember that first spoonful of the wet, dark-brown stew, with delicious chewy lumps, small bits of vegetables—some of them orange, which tasted quite sweet (later on I learned that they were reconstituted dried sweet potatoes, all the way from distant America). I had never tasted anything so wonderful. Every cell in my body seemed to reach out for this nourishment. When I got to the bottom of the canteen, I noticed how tight my midsection felt; a full stomach was something new to me. About an hour later I had cramps and felt slightly nauseous, but fought hard not to vomit. I was not going to lose such a meal!

When I got home that afternoon, I told Mother about the incredible experience. By then my skinny little body was eagerly digesting the amazing food. Mother started to cry for joy and blessed the Americans. She told me that they came from a country where people were kind and generous and had lots of space and all got on with one another. They had liberated Europe, and we were alive because of them. Mother's glowing description made a lasting impression on me, and I took in every word of it.

As the school year progressed, our new friends continued to come to the school every day, with milk, fruit, and other stews, like chicken with peas and carrots. I learned to eat more slowly, and sometimes I went back for seconds to take some home for my mother, who, at thirty-seven years old, looked like a beanstalk, so thin was she. The American soldiers became supermen in my imagination. They appeared to come from another galaxy. I had been told that America was on the other side of the world, but for me it was easier to look up into the night sky and imagine this land of loving brotherhood with its gleaming cities and happy people, just slightly to the left of the full moon.

The black soldier from that first day and I became friends. One day he picked me up as if I was light as a feather and put some packets in my coat pocket. One of my teachers became alarmed, ran toward us, and pulled me away, telling me never to get that close again to a *Neger* (black person). I did not understand why and was confused. I showed one of the packets I had received to the girl who sat next to me in class. She had seen something like that before and explained that it was *Kaugummi* (chewing gum) and that you could chew it forever and ever. So after school we did, and I took the rest home with me and shared it with my sisters.

In December class was rehearsing for our part in the school Christmas play. We were all going to be angels. I really wanted to be a shepherd, especially as I felt not worthy to be an angel with all my sins, but the teacher told me in no uncertain terms that only boys could be shepherds. So there was nothing to be done. Mother made me a white tunic out of a sheet and painted silver stars all over it with leftover silver paint that she had used to cover the stovepipe in our winter quarters.

We learned to sing "Silent Night, Holy Night" in harmony and many other carols. For the final dress rehearsal, Mother braided gold and silver ribbons into my hair. It looked quite angelic, and I was reconciled to playing an angel. The dress rehearsal turned out to be the best part of our festivities, as our American benefactors came.

They looked even taller sitting in rows on our small chairs, with their long legs stretched out before them. From up on the stage I was able to look at them closely. They really looked as if they had come from another world. Their skin was shiny as was their hair, short and often sticking straight up, looking more like soft fur. I noticed how beautifully shaped their teeth were and how white, and when they moved it was with such relaxed grace.

Some of them wiped away tears when we started to sing. Did they think of their own home, their faraway world, the families they had to leave behind to be here and help us? And where was this world, this "Shangri-La," this *Amerika?* And then it hit me. That world must be close to where the star of Bethlehem had appeared so long ago, way up in the sky. These tall and handsome saviors had come from there to help us. I got quite choked up at the enormity of my findings and could hardly continue to sing. This impression stayed with me for many years, and I saw every American I met through those specially tinted Christmas glasses.

The dress rehearsal went well and everyone was in high spirits, even the normally stern-looking headmaster. My Negro friend brought out a trumpet and played an American Christmas song, which thirty years later I discovered was written by Irving Berlin in 1942 and was called "White Christmas." Then our soldier friends opened big boxes and gave everyone a small wrapped gift, as well as a toothbrush and a white tube. I had never seen a toothbrush before and could not see the point of it, as I had no hair on my teeth.

On my way home I unwrapped the gift; it was a small bear with a red Santa Claus hat. I loved it! But the toothpaste intrigued me the most. I unscrewed the top and squeezed some on my hand; it smelled good, so I licked it. The taste was sweet and had a distinct aroma. Years later, in the 1960s, when my children let me try some of their bubble gum, I immediately connected the flavor to my first toothpaste experience.

By the time I came home I had eaten all but a tiny bit of the full-size tube. I showed mother my Christmas bear, the toothbrush with the blue and yellow handle, and the sorry remnants of the toothpaste. Mother was not pleased. "This would have lasted us for at least six months; how could you?" was her only response. Later my sister Gabi explained to me what the brush and tube were intended for. Now I understood and felt ashamed for my greediness and gluttony, yet further proof that I was a hopeless sinner. But the next day Mother laughed about it as we proceeded to use the toothbrush with ordinary hand soap, which was all right as long as one rinsed out thoroughly afterward.

My love affair with America and her people had begun. Their influence and presence, generosity and selfless giving, as well as their lightness of being, would become a bright beacon through my younger years and would finally bring me to this "faraway planet," this America, for which I yearned for so many long years.

CHAPTER 14

Agnus Dei
Qui tollis peccata mundi,
Miserere nobis.

Lamb of God
Who takes away the sins of the world,
Have mercy upon us.
                    —Catholic Liturgical Mass, based on John 1:29

And so my education continued. Another thing I discovered was that not everybody was a Catholic. We were Catholics. Mother had become one, rather reluctantly, in order to be able to marry my father in 1933. My paternal grandmother de Werth had converted from the Protestant faith to Catholicism after her husband's death. He, Clemens de Werth, an architect, had been part of a family whose roots dated back to the Huguenots, who played a part in the French Revolution. Grandmother, like many converts, became quite fanatical. She had a chapel built at their mansion in Kleve, on the Dutch border, where Mass was celebrated daily. The six children, two girls and four boys (my father being the youngest), were brought up in the strictest Jesuit tradition—daily Mass, confession, and the whole nine yards.

Father had obviously rebelled against this strict regime. The only remnants of it that he preserved were keeping the main holidays and seeing to it that his daughters were brought up in the faith. Before his mother's death, the whole estate was transferred to the Catholic Church, so Father's share of the inheritance was lost in any case.

Sabina's grandfather,
Arthur Maskus (*Opi*), 1906

Omi and *Opi*, 1918

Mother, by contrast, had been raised by a man, my grandfather Arthur, who was the head of the *Freidenker* (literally, freethinkers) for the whole of Germany. The freethinkers originated in England and France in the 1700s. By 1850 they had a large following in Germany, and in the 1920s they really thrived in the defeated Germany and later in opposition to the Nazis.

The freethinkers were not affiliated with any established religion; in fact, they stood against church dogma, although they weren't atheists either. They believed in scientific knowledge and classical education and stood for freedom, equality, tolerance, and renunciation of all violence. This meant that they were opposed to any kind of militarism and fascism. Because of this philosophy they were very vulnerable to persecution by the Hitler regime.

Grandfather Arthur Maskus fought for Germany in the First World War. As a lieutenant in his early thirties, he saw terrible fighting, mostly on the western front, and came back to my grandmother Magdalena a different man, more serious and determined to do everything possible to avoid another such catastrophe. He threw himself heart and soul into the freethinker organization and still managed to provide for his wife and three children by running a small upholstery business in Görlitz, Silesia. He passed on his philosophy of life to his children.

In the middle of February 1933, his youngest daughter, Margareta, found her father unconscious in the basement of their house, bleeding from several head wounds. With her mother's help, she carried him upstairs, and the family nursed him around the clock. They were too scared to take him to the hospital. On February 23, he died at the age of forty-seven. Grandmother mourned his death for the rest of her life.

Mother often talked about him; she had been very close to him. He had been a very warm and enthusiastic person, an autodidact, and very inventive in a practical sense. His death certificate said he had died from a wound to the head after he fell down the cellar stairs. In fact he was beaten close to death with a sharp instrument by some Nazi thugs.

A year later Hitler banned all freethinker associations, causing many to go underground and fight in the resistance. Grandfather's successor, Max Sievens, was caught and jailed in Brandenburg and executed there on January 17, 1944.

My mother, Klara, or, Klarissa, as she liked to be called, was devastated by her father's violent death. Her relationship with her mother was not particularly good, and living at home was now difficult. She had also suffered another painful loss just a few months before. Her fiancé, Wolfgang, a doctor's son who lived in a small town nearby, was tragically killed in a motorcycle accident while on the way to see her.

Her main objective now was to get away from home. She was just twenty-two, and she sought a new life that might help her get over the two losses. So when my father came along with his charm and "understanding," she ignored the warning signs and agreed to marry him on May 3, 1933. She poured all her love and soul into the marriage, and two and a half years later my oldest sister, Gabriele, was born.

I learned a lot from my mother's philosophy about tolerance and self-expression, which gave me somewhat of a buffer against the very

Grandfather before his assassination

Mother in the early 1930s

dogmatic religious instruction we received at school. Going to church, however, was really quite nice. Germany has many religious holidays, and Mother saw to it that we were well dressed and did not look like refugees. Father had bought a secondhand sewing machine for her, and, being resourceful, she found material to create beautiful dresses, skirts, and blouses—all the same style and fabric but in three different sizes.

One Christmas she made us three beautiful winter coats out of some olive-green army blankets, which she had dyed dark navy blue in the basement water boiler. They had large pockets, were double-breasted, with big white mother-of-pearl buttons and white starched collars over the wool collar, which could be unbuttoned and washed as needed. The inside she lined with some curtains in gold damask satin. We looked like princesses—eight, eleven, and fourteen years old!

Mother only went to church on Christmas Eve for the midnight Mass. Father went even less often. If he was home at all, he slept through Sunday mornings, as he was usually out on Saturday night until the early hours. So we three girls made quite an entrance in the church, parading in on our own. It was a far cry from the way we must have looked just a few years before.

The best thing about church was the music and the singing. I soon caught on to the medieval hymns, which had a melancholy sound. I did not understand most of the words, but I could feel the suffering in them, and of course everywhere I looked were statues and pictures of the suffering Jesus or some saint who had been martyred. I tried to imagine how much it would hurt to be nailed to a cross through your hands and your feet with no food or water, only vinegar. I felt close to Jesus when I looked up at him.

The Mass back then was in Latin, and I tried very hard to make some sense of the words. I heard the phrase *Dominus vobis cum* (The Lord be with you) as if it were German, *Dominus, wo bist du?* (Lord, where are you?). This struck me as a very odd question, especially as it was repeated many times during the service. Wasn't God supposed to be right here, in his own house? And if the priest had to ask so many times and got no answer, we were really in trouble.

A LONG SILENCE

I also discovered that I was a miserable sinner. The list was long: forgetting my morning prayers most days, having bad thoughts, not liking all the kids or teachers at school, getting joy out of looking at myself in the mirror and finding that I was very pretty, feeling envy for others, and being greedy when it came to food. This was the beginning of my inner struggle against sinning, as the church taught me, and the inevitable feeling of guilt over my transgressions, which I was convinced were a great disappointment to Jesus Christ.

CHAPTER 15

They dined on mince, and slices of quince,
Which they ate with a runcible spoon;
And hand in hand, on the edge of the sand,
They danced by the light of the moon.
> —Edward Lear (1812–1888),
> from "The Owl and the Pussycat" (1871)

Only a few refugee children were in my class, most of them from the east, like me. They spoke in a variety of accents and dialects compared to the majority, who were Swabian girls and had their own way of speaking, using local words, word endings, and different grammar not found in our German reader. I was brought up to speak *Hochdeutsch* (high German), which is nearly accent-free and uses grammatically correct German—the German equivalent of an upper-class, or "BBC," British accent. My way of speaking must have made me seem slightly arrogant, but my teachers loved it, and I was often chosen to read aloud, especially at school events, to recite poems and ballads, and so on. I liked it, especially as it gave me some status.

Being labeled a refugee was not always very pleasant. We got teased a lot and told we were dirty, full of lice and other vermin; worst of all, we were called *Pack*, meaning the lowest form of humanity. In English one would say "trash" or "baggage." I just wanted to be a normal kid and not get handouts and be made to feel different or less of a person. I wanted to belong, and yet I could not. In writing these pages, I am aware now that I never felt at home in Germany, nor did I feel a shred of national pride.

A LONG SILENCE

Most of the adults in my immediate life were very kind to my family and me. Herr Neuwirth, our landlord, became my special friend. I had found out that he was a Protestant, which was very puzzling to me, as he seemed like such a nice man. One day, while he was feeding his chickens, I went up to him and said, "Herr Neuwirth, you are a Protestant, aren't you?" When he nodded, I added, "So your chickens must be Protestants too, yes?" His face changed into a beautiful smile as he explained that animals were a part of creation that was good, and therefore they did not need any religion to stop them from committing sins—only people did. This made a lot of sense to me, as I knew all about sinning. I started to envy animals from then on.

In those years, we had a family doctor who lived just around the corner. Dr. Neuffer was a grandfatherly man who made house calls. We kept him busy, as we were sick a lot. Whether it was chicken pox, measles, swollen tonsils, ear infections, stomach flu, or real influenza, he appeared at our bedside, stroking our hair, telling funny stories, bringing quinine pills, lozenges, and an unshakable conviction that we would be better quite soon. He was always right.

One sixth of December, Saint Nicholas Day, he came dressed as the saint and was recognizable only by the tone and kindness of his voice. He brought us nuts, apples, and sweet cookies that his wife had baked for us.

When Mother was ill with her frequent gallbladder attacks, vomiting and looking yellow for days on end, or when she was so distressed she would just lie in bed not responding to anything, we could quickly walk up Waldstrasse and leave a message for the good doctor to come and see Mother, which he did after his work at the hospital. Maybe he prescribed some pills to help her sleep better; anyhow, she would get well again after his long visits, during which they talked a lot.

I was very scared of these episodes, but then I was scared of so many things. There were many desperate people around who had trouble adjusting to a more lawful life after the chaos of the war. Many murders occurred, and burglaries were common. Twice someone tried to come into our house. Once when I was home alone, a man climbed through the window into the kitchen area. I froze in terror and stared at him so fiercely that he turned and left the way he had come in.

But the worst fear of mine developed after I overheard a conversation between two women in front of me at the bakery. One was warning the other not to buy any more canned pork from the black market, as fingers of babies and children had been found in some. I felt sick imagining it and blurted my findings out to Mother when I got home. She brushed it off as pure nonsense, telling me something like "that could never happen." But I did not believe her, especially after a neighborhood boy told me that humans taste like pork.

Now my long walk to school became a nightmare. I had to walk through a part of the old town, down narrow streets enclosed by four-story apartment houses. School started at 8 a.m. sharp, so during the winter months it was still dark, and it was easy to imagine "children snatchers" rushing out of dark doorways to catch me to make more human pork. Mostly I tried to leave the house early enough so that I could meet up with other kids I knew.

But one morning I was a bit late, and no children were around. The scary street went uphill and, as there was no traffic, I walked in the middle of the street. Suddenly a man came rushing out of one of the doors diagonally toward me. I started to run as fast as I could and took the next turn into an unfamiliar street, which turned out to be a cul-de-sac. I dared not turn back or even look back, so I ran through a garden gate and hid in the bushes. It was a long time before I found the nerve to stick my head up to see if the man had followed me. Eventually I ventured out and hastened to school.

I was terribly late, and the teacher was not pleased. She took me into the hallway and insisted that I tell her why I could not get to school on time, all the while giving me scary, penetrating looks. I broke down in tears and told her about my narrow escape. And this elderly lady, who deserved a prize for being so skillful in entering a child's mind, said the only thing that could have diminished my fear: "Oh, Sabina, you need never be worried about being snatched and made into food. You are too thin; you wouldn't even be good for soup." Well, this settled my fears once and for all. The logic of it was overwhelming, and from then on I marched to and from school with confidence and self-assurance.

Even though my fear of cannibalism had subsided, I remember an underlying climate of imminent danger. Mother, who was always vigilant and fearful, projected her own feelings onto us, especially onto Tina and me. We were both very tense and jumpy and had terrible nightmares. Tina would often sleepwalk, and we had to look for her in the morning, mostly in confined spaces; we'd find her squeezed behind a piece of furniture, curled up like a contortionist, fast asleep.

The effects of war go on for so many years, often for generations, and long after the peace treaties have been signed. In war, all are victims. What kind of lives did the German soldiers, even the ones in the *Waffen* SS, lead after the war? How did they sleep at night or forget what they had been part of?

Food, the lack of it, and how to get it were the foremost thoughts in people's minds in the immediate years after the war had ended. During the month of May, hordes of schoolchildren went out to collect maybugs, the shiny brown oval beetles the size of half an adult thumb. These creatures fed voraciously on beech leaves. There were lots of beech trees in the parks and woods, as well as beech-hedges around many houses, so it was easy to pick them off the lower branches and put them in boxes with lids, cooking pots, or any container that could be covered, with some air going in, to keep the insects alive. Special collection depots were set up, and from there farmers would pick up the "crop" to feed to their chickens. It was quite common to find a wing or leg segment of a maybeetle in an egg yolk.

In the autumn many people went into the municipal parks and woods to gather beechnuts that had ripened and fallen to the ground, before rats and squirrels ate them all. The nuts were taken to a pressing station. If my family picked all day, we would get about one cup of beechnut oil, which was very precious and used sparingly for cooking.

Along the roadside and in meadows we would dig up chicory plants. They had tall woody stalks with pale-blue starburst flowers, but it was the long taproots we were after. Mother roasted the cut-up roots in a saucepan and then ground them up with a manual coffee grinder. It made an extremely bitter brew, only slightly reminiscent of coffee. By this time, dark brown syrup made from sugar beet was available, and I learned to love it. It made our "coffee" easier to drink.

During October we had two weeks of harvest vacation. That meant being out on the stubble fields picking up any grain that had not been raked up and having it ground up into flour. We could also walk over the potato fields and look for small potatoes that had been left behind. An old farmhouse with a big yard had a sauerkraut-making operation. Small mountains of cone-shaped white cabbages were cut up with a special machine, and the tough middle would shoot out on one end into a large heap. We could take as many of these thick stalks as we wanted. They were tough and hard but tasted wonderfully sweet. We would eat them right there, sitting on the ground, grating away pieces with our small teeth, like raccoons or squirrels, only our teeth were not as strong and efficient. I lost one of my first baby incisors during our cabbage feast. I carried my little backpack, filled with cabbage centers, home to the delight of my mother. She would boil them slowly with vinegar, water, and caraway seeds. What a treat this was!

When meat was available in a store, we did not ask what kind of meat it was. I know we ate horse and whale meat and something my mother referred to as roof rabbit. One day at school I learned by acci-dent what we had been eating. In nature studies the teacher asked us what kind of rabbits we knew. I raised my hand and said, "Roof rabbits," which live on roofs. The teacher said she had never heard of rabbits living on roofs; maybe I was confusing them with squirrels. But I insisted and told the whole class that you could eat them. Some of the students began to snigger and whisper among themselves, and it was then that I discovered we had been eating domestic cats. I was disgusted and angry at my mother for not telling us the truth. But, had she done so, I would not have eaten the tender meat and would have remained starved for protein.

Years later, in Vietnam I saw very cute midsize dogs, chubby with thick fur and adorable faces, being transported to the market for food in large baskets strapped to the back of bicycles. I look at our beautiful gray-spotted Maine Coon cat, Amanda Blake, a member of our family, and I hope she cannot read this and find out that I was something of a cannibal in my youth.

CHAPTER 16

Each friend represents a world in us;
a world possibly not born until they arrive,
and it is only in meeting them that a new world is born.
—Anaïs Nin (1903–1977), *The Diary of Anaïs Nin*, Vol. 1

When school was out, I could walk to the very end of Silberpappelweg, stop at a pretty brick house with a gable, a cherry tree on one side, and high pines on the other, and ask my school friend Eva Ricker to come out and play with me. On nice days we spent hours at the edge of the forest and built small houses with sticks, bark from different trees, moss, and acorns for a world of imaginary elves and dwarfs. I remember the long drawn-out summer days under the trees, the dappled sunlight trying to come through the canopy, as we were building small elfin villages with a magnificent structure in the middle for the elf queen. The roofs were made with slabs of oak and pine bark, and inside we created furniture, carpets, sofas, armchairs upholstered in moss, beds with emerald green pillows and comforters woven out of summer grasses, out of which stuck just a little elf hat, made from an acorn pod. The dwarf village was less refined; here we would make small dens with sticks and leaves and rough tables and benches.

Mother knew that I was in good hands at the Rickers'. Eva's parents treated me as if I was another daughter. There were two nearly grown-up brothers, both away at university, so Eva had an ideal playmate in me. In appearance she was the exact opposite of me, with her thick dark-brown hair, her prominent bushy eyebrows, and eyes the color of shiny dark cherries. We were the same height, but Eva had a strong, solid body. She already played tennis, skied, and on weekends sailed with her brothers on Lake Constance on their small yacht.

We two eight-year-olds loved each other very much and pretended to be sisters; even Frau Ricker called us *Rosen Rot und Rosen Weiss* (Rose Red and Rose White) after two maidens in a German fairy tale. The Rickers' house was a real home, with a happy father and mother, a cozy kitchen, and a wood-paneled breakfast room complete with corner bench, colorful cushions, and a green-tiled built-in stove. Then there was a music room with a grand piano and various instruments. The entrance hall was enormous, with two Oriental carpets, a little sitting area, and a lovely carpeted staircase with carved wooden banisters leading to the second floor.

Eva had her very own bedroom upstairs, a spacious room with windows on two walls, so it was bright even on rainy days. There was a large bookshelf filled with books, a big cupboard for toys, and many wonderful dolls, which I liked the best. She had many dolls' clothes and small suitcases for them. One of our favorite games was to bathe the dolls, in Eva's own bathroom, with hot and cold running water. Then we would get them dressed for a trip, pack the small suitcases, and pretend we were two mothers going on vacation with our children or escaping the bombing. I have a feeling I set the agenda for our imaginary trips, in my unconscious attempt to rework my own experiences, to try to gain control over them and have a better outcome this time.

In our play we would go down to the first floor, where we would arrange the chairs in the large formal dining room like the benches in a train, or we would knock on the door of the room in the back of the house. A very old lady, a Baltic German from Reval, Estonia, occupied the room. She was a refugee like me and had been adopted into the Ricker family, as she had lost all her own family to the Russians. She was hard to understand but had such kind light-blue eyes and expressive hands that we loved to visit her. She always joined our pretend travels, as we visited castles and other great places in the country and had picnics on the banks of imaginary rivers with our doll children.

Often I was invited to stay for lunch, which in Germany is the main meal of the day. I loved these plentiful, delicious meals served by the Rickers' household maid, who was not much older than my sister Gabi, but who treated me with such courtesy and respect that I felt like a princess. Then in the afternoons we played board games, or Eva practiced on the piano and her violin for her upcoming lesson. I was fascinated, so Eva would let me try the piano, which I loved. I would make up little slow tunes, using the black keys quite a bit, because it sounded so melancholy.

Around five o'clock the front door would open and Herr Ricker would walk in. While putting down his big briefcase he called out, "Where are my two little girls?" And with that he'd swoop us both up, one on each side, and laugh and ask us about our latest adventures, calling for hot cocoa to be brought into the breakfast room. From his briefcase emerged a brown paper bag with pretzels, still warm from the baker's oven. What a feast we had; sometimes we even had a bit of real butter, which tasted heavenly. My idea of what a father could be changed dramatically, especially when he hugged his wife in front of us. Herr Ricker was one of the directors of AEG, a company that made electrical appliances, like stoves, refrigerators, water heaters, washing machines, and more, something like GE in the United States. I gathered that he and his family had suffered relatively little during the war, even though in 1953 they lost their oldest son, Johannes, to leukemia. Mother remarked at the time that tragedy spares no one.

During the Christmas holidays the entire basement of Eva's house was transformed into a model-railway paradise. Over many years her father and the boys had built up a beautiful and realistic train network, with tunnels going through doorways and emerging from the alpine regions of a snowy mountainous country into a beautiful green place with palm trees and blue lakes. Eva and I were not allowed to touch the complicated controls, which directed many trains, both passenger and freight trains moving coal, wood, and cattle, around a labyrinth of tracks. But just watching it in motion was totally mesmerizing.

It was a happy house from top to bottom, so going back home at the end of the day was always a hard transition. My own family was so different. Gabi, who was now fourteen years old, had filled out and might just as well have lived on another planet. She had a short temper, and I kept out of her way as much as possible. Tina, now eleven, was withdrawn and had few friends, young or old. I think she trusted no one, and people, even her teachers, found her hard to engage. But she was kind, and I loved her very much, even though I did not know how to make life easier for her.

One morning, when we got up to get ready for school, Mother was nowhere to be found. She often left before first light to look for mushrooms but was usually back before we were dressed. Just before I needed to leave for school, Mother came through the terrace doors, wet and muddy and very upset. She told me that she had been out early to pick up apples in a nearby orchard, after the night's heavy storm, and was arrested by two policemen for trespassing and stealing and then taken to the police station. Eventually they let her go, but Mother felt humiliated and angry, because she had to leave her bounty behind. I tried to imagine Frau Ricker doing something like that and realized we were refugees and poor, no matter what. As I hurried to school, I felt a great sense of shame.

CHAPTER 17

**And in the sweetness of friendship let
there be laughter, and sharing of pleasures.
For in the dew of little things the heart
finds its morning and is refreshed.**
—Kahlil Gibran (1883–1931),
"On Friendship," from *The Prophet* (1923)

B y now everyone had ration cards and the food situation had
improved. We had very little cash to buy anything that was available on the black market. Any kind of fat was difficult to come by, and
our ration cards allowed just a few ounces of pork fat per month, which
made cooking quite a challenge. Standing in a long line at the butcher's
one day, Mother got into a conversation with three very funny and
unusual men, all of them were in their late thirties like her. After about
an hour in line, they all decided to pool their meager resources so she
could make a large pot of potato soup with bits of pork rind and fat as
well as onions. The men would bring all their bread rations, and one of
them knew where to get a bottle of red wine and maybe a small piece
of cheese. It was all arranged.

Two days later, the three arrived, bearing gifts like the three kings
in the Bible. They entered our place singing and in such good spirits
that at first we children were quite taken aback. But they soon infected
us with their liveliness, and we learned that they were artist friends.
One of them wore a black beret and had a magnificent chestnut-colored
moustache, which made him look like a smiling seal. His name was
Helmut Bibow (pronounced bee-bo), and he wanted to be called Bibow,

The three artists

Bibow, Gabi, Lilo, and Sabina, 1949

so we children called him *Onkel* Bibow. Another man had graying curly hair, quite long, and a mottled full beard, which gave him the appearance of a young Santa Claus. The third had longish brown hair, swept back, and he sat with his arms crossed and the most wonderful smile on his face, even when he was talking.

My mother came to life in their presence in a way I had never seen before. The three new "uncles" teased her: "Legendary Klarissa, where is your famous potato soup that we have heard so much about? We are starving painters and have been dreaming about this night for days!" Wine was produced and a corkscrew, and then I had my first sip of red wine. I liked the grown-up taste. Mother brought out the steaming pot of soup, sprinkled with green parsley, and *Onkel* Bibow followed behind with the heated bread.

What a feast we had that night on the terrace! Mother forgot all about keeping the noise down as we normally did so Frau Neuwirth would not complain. We laughed, and the men told funny stories, feeding off each other's wit, and Mother's eyes were sparkling like black cherries after a summer rain. All seemed right with the world that evening; even Tina was animated and smiled a lot.

We would have many more evenings like that in the summer of 1949, but eventually *Onkel* Bibow would come by himself. His friends, whose names I can no longer recall, had moved away. "Santa Claus" immigrated to California, where he would become a successful set designer for one of the big studios in Hollywood. He designed and built the model of Moby-Dick, the whale that haunted Captain Ahab portrayed by Gregory Peck in the adaptation of Herman Melville's novel *Moby-Dick*.

Onkel Bibow became like a real uncle to us over time, which was especially nice since Father was gone so much and we had hardly any male presence in the house. Bibow would entertain us with wild stories, and while talking, he would sketch the characters on large pieces of paper with a fountain pen. He could draw everything backward. For instance, he once started with a tail and ended with a perfect elephant, atop which sat a cross-legged man in a turban. On another occasion, he

Father and Mother

Bibow's drawing of announcement of change of address

drew while telling the story of Don Quixote. First came the horse, Rocinante; then the knight in full armor, boots first; this was followed by some torn old shoes some distance away, which developed stroke by stroke into his servant, Sancho Panza. Bibow was a fabulous illustrator.

He was also the most eccentric un-German person one could imagine. He lived above an old run-down inn at the edge of some woods, where it always appeared as if it were dusk and raining, so overgrown was the outside of the building. He lived there all by himself after leaving Berlin in 1945, when the Russians began their approach. He painted and drew until late at night when the ghosts came visiting him, as he would say. Much of his art was a satirical expression of his political views and the human condition.

We all visited him one Sunday afternoon. His bedroom was so damp and moldy that he had nailed huge toadstools, pulled off tree trunks outside, onto his mahogany wardrobe where they continued to grow around the peeling veneer. For some reason this made a great impression on me, as did one of the paintings leaning against the wall. As the bombs were falling in Berlin, Bibow had painted a street scene, using the ashes of burned buildings for paint, in gray, black, and reddish tones. All one could see was the ground of rusty red ashes and in the background the skeletons of what remained of high buildings. In the center of the painting a gray arm had broken through the scorched earth and a hand was holding the receiver of a black telephone toward the gray sky. I have never forgotten this picture and the desolation it expressed.

Then one day *Onkel* Bibow came to visit accompanied by a young, shapely red-haired woman. His new love was named Lilo (Leelo), and from then on it was Bibow and Lilo. She had a huge bosom, displayed in a rather revealing, clinging dress and squeezed into a very pointed brassiere. This produced a striking impression in contrast with her otherwise slim figure, like two mountain peaks jutting out. She wore bright red lipstick and laughed a lot, showing us her slightly protruding white teeth. She would become Bibow's prototype for all the women in his drawings from then on. Bibow had found his muse.

Bibow kissing
Mother's hand

I had rather hoped that if my father disappeared altogether, *Onkel* Bibow could marry my mother, the "legendary Klarissa," and we would live happily ever after with much laughter and endless storytelling. Luckily, *Onkel* Bibow stayed a loyal friend, with the buxom Lilo in tow; he was nice to Father on the rare occasions he was around and continued to admire my mother. He was a very good friend to her, especially after my father actually left us.

This happened at the beginning of December 1950, when Father decided to set up house and a men's clothing shop with one of his colleagues from work, a Frau Roggentin, with whom he was having a long-standing affair. Just before Christmas of that year, my mother had a complete nervous breakdown and ended up in a hospital after another suicide attempt. *Onkel* Bibow was away, but when he found out he sent a wonderful drawing to her in the hospital. It was very simple; he had drawn a heart broken in two and above it a tube of glue with two drops falling between the two halves to mend it. Mother told me years later that this drawing became a lifeline, providing a glimmer of hope and helping her to eventually recover. I am reminded of the last few lines of

Bibow's drawing of his room above a restaurant

Bibow's pencil drawing of an elephant

One of Bibow's many pen-and-ink drawings of a scene in Corsica

a poem, "The Lightest Touch," by the contemporary poet and visionary David Whyte, in which he says:

> You can feel Lazarus
> deep inside
> even the laziest, most deathly afraid
> part of you,
> lift up his hands and walk toward the light.

The miracle was, from then on, Mother did walk toward the light.

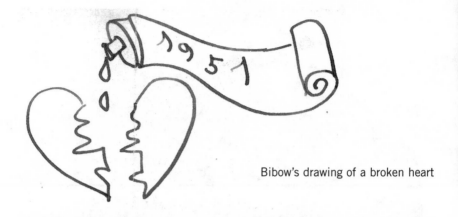

Bibow's drawing of a broken heart

FRÖHLICHE WEIHNACHTEN
UND DIE BESTEN WÜNSCHE
ZUM NEUEN JAHR!

Helmut Bibow · Stuttgart · Alexanderstraße 137

Onkel Bibow became a very well-known and successful illustrator and political satirist. He illustrated the works of his friend, the German writer and poet Rudolf Hagelstange, then a book on the lives of dinosaurs and early humans, in which some of the scantily clad women resembled his Lilo, whom he had married. By this time, he could afford to move into better quarters, so he and Lilo left Stuttgart to settle outside of Hamburg with their black cat, Lumumba. Later they moved to Bavaria and lived on the shores of Starnberger See in a large old rambling farmhouse. Bibow kept in touch with us until the early sixties. In 1973, he collapsed suddenly and died of a heart attack.

CHAPTER 18

The solid mountains shone, bright as the clouds,
Grain-tinctured, drenched in empyrean light;
And in the meadows and the lower grounds
Was all the sweetness of a common dawn—
— William Wordsworth (1770–1850),
from "Summer Vacation, The Prelude,"
Book IV, *Complete Poetical Works* (1888)

During Mother's hospitalization, my sisters and I were split up very suddenly. I was sent by train to what turned out to be a magical place in the Austrian Alps, to Mittelberg, Klein Walsertal, a valley ringed by magnificent snowcapped mountains. I stayed in the home of the Stingele family, Hans and Udi, who lived in a very large three-hundred-year-old wooden mountain chalet, up a steep slope, opposite the village of Mittelberg. Their house, which had been converted into a children's home (*Kinderhaus*), could only be reached on foot or on skis. One had to cross a ramshackle covered footbridge that spanned the roaring mountain river Breitach and then hike upward along a serpentine path. The luggage and all sorts of supplies, including food, came across on a primitive cable car, dangling and swinging from side to side between high firs and poles. I had never seen anything like it.

For the first two days I was a bit homesick, especially as I did not know whether Mother would get better or whether she might die. And what had happened to my sisters? As it turned out, they were being looked after by my widowed and childless aunt Marga, Mother's sister, and by *Omi*, our grandmother. They had both escaped from East Germany early in 1950 and were living near Stuttgart.

Kinderhaus am Hohenwald (Children's Home at the High Forest)

Harald Stingele, the ski instructor

But it did not take me long before I felt at home in this peaceful place. I had a lovely wooden bed to sleep in with a soft, blue-and-white-checkered featherbed (comforter) and two matching pillows. From there I could look out on the mountains. I shared the room with two other girls my own age, and we were very cozy in the wood-paneled room. Down the hallway was a big bathroom, with a long row of sinks. One of the sinks had "Sabina" written above it, and I had my own tooth mug and a large tube of toothpaste all to myself. Brushing my teeth in this splendor and having hot and cold water available whenever I wanted gave me enormous pleasure.

There was a curtain at one end, which led to several shiny new bathtubs, where we were given baths twice a week in clean firsthand water. There were about a dozen other children like me, boys and girls, some younger and a few older ones, as well as the Stingele's three sons. Their youngest, Harald, was a beautiful boy, with chestnut-colored hair bleached in streaks by the mountain sun; he was our ski instructor for the next two weeks. Despite being only nine years old, he was an accomplished and graceful skier and taught us the basics in a few days. Skiing was the only way to get around when the snow was deep. The middle brother, Alwig, made a great impression on me when he played the cello for us. His concentration was so complete that when he got to a difficult passage, his tongue would come out and follow the direction in which he was moving the bow. The oldest, Volkart, was mostly away at school and then at medical school in Munich. He later became the object of my first romantic love.

On one of my first mornings there, snow was quietly falling outside and all the fir trees looked dressed for Christmas in their white coats. We awoke to the smell of hot chocolate and toasted bread wafting up from downstairs, a delicious enticement to get ready quickly. No sooner had our young female assistants—we called them *Tanten* (aunties)—combed and braided our hair, than we ran downstairs to the largest room of the house, where an enormous round table was set up with chairs all around. There our new temporary parents welcomed us to a real feast.

We started with a bowl of muesli, the likes of which I have never been able to duplicate since, nor was it like the muesli you can buy in stores today. It consisted of oats, nuts, raisins, sultanas, pieces of apples and pears, cinnamon, and who knows what else, expanded into a delicious crunchy mush in thick yellow buttermilk. I had never had anything but skimmed, watery milk before, so this was a new experience. My belly grew under my sweater. The hot cocoa was intoxicating, followed by warm crusty white bread, which one could spread with real golden butter and strawberry jam made with whole strawberries from the previous summer, still intact.

I had already made friends with a girl, Ruth, who sat next to me. Normally I was very chatty, but she could not get a peep out of me during the whole sensuous meal, so absorbed was I in the experience.

After breakfast we had our first ski lesson. We were given square-toed leather boots, thick woolen socks, long warm pants, anoraks, and wooden skis together with poles. To choose the correct length of skis, one had to raise one arm with outstretched hand. The correct length was from feet to fingertips. The skis were narrow, no more than three to four inches wide, and our boots came up to just above the anklebone. The poles were made of hazelnut branches with metal tips; near the bottom was a wheel with leather spokes, and at the top was a leather loop for the wrist and a leather grip. We were shown how to wax the skis, which would stop the snow from sticking and make them glide better.

Finally it was time to go outside. The snow had stopped, and I was dazzled by the deepest blue sky I had ever seen. Even though it was December, I could feel the strength of the sun. The house was at an elevation of four thousand feet, and in the clear atmosphere the sun was powerful. Big chunks of white powdery snow blew off the giant spruce trees every now and then, where a slight breeze would catch and transform them into a bridal veil for a short time, until they grew thinner and thinner and finally disappeared altogether.

Putting on the skis was easy. You just let your boots slide into the metal fitting, brought the clamp up over the toe section, and pulled it back on each side with metal levers, which fit into the heel section of the contraption. Staying upright with these long foot extensions was a lot more difficult. Our able ski instructor, Harald, started us off gliding forward, one leg at a time, and by the end of the morning, we could stand on a gentle slope and move forward, with knees bent, bottoms out, and sticks behind us. There was much laughter when we tumbled into the soft snow and tried to stand up again. Harald showed us the correct and only way to do this, without making "ski salad," and also demonstrated how to walk uphill, skis out at a wide angle, weight forward.

That was it for the first day. We took the skies off at the back door, wiped them, and put them in the ski racks, each of which was marked with a child's name. In the mudroom we hung up our socks and set the boots out to dry, as well as our other garments. As a reward there was hot milk and toasted bread with golden bubbling cheese waiting for us.

A little later we marched out in single file along a shoveled path to a structure as big as a barn, with a sloping roof and no wall on the southern side; this was the *Liege Halle* (nap room). There on a wooden platform were a row of army cots, with pillows and thick blankets on each, inviting us to take a well-deserved rest. One of the "aunts," Ingrid, started reading to us the story of little Nils Holgerssons by Selma Lagerlöf, a boy who longed to fly with the wild geese, and did, on their yearly migration to faraway places. The story described the society of these geese, their adventures and tragedies, and the beauty of the world seen from high above.

The sun shone on us, and I pushed the blanket down to my feet; it seemed warm like in the summertime. I listened to *Tante* Ingrid's voice, but after awhile I heard only the wind in the trees, and even that became fainter as I entered into a sleep so deep and delicious, a sleep without any tension or fear, where my body and soul just let go in a way I had never experienced before.

When I resurfaced I thought I was flying on the back of a goose, like little Nils Holgerssons, that's how light my body felt. The other children stirred, and soon we all went back to the house to wash up and come down to the midday meal.

I could not believe the abundance of food. It was like in a fairy story, like waking up in the land of milk and honey. Despite not feeling as ravenous as I normally felt before a meal, after the breakfast and snack, my appetite was restored as soon as my nose picked up the smell of roast chicken and gravy, and I saw the glistening carrots and browned potatoes. I even had room for the dessert, tapioca pudding with stewed dried fruit, made from apricots, prunes, and figs with a touch of cinnamon.

After the meal we had quiet time. I was still quite sleepy, and my extended belly had work to do, so I crept into my cozy bed upstairs for another nap.

At three o'clock I was awakened and joined the others downstairs in a schoolroom where we were assigned tasks depending on our level of education. Writing, math, reading something and then describing it, and learning chapters in books about geography, biology, and history were some of our assignments. To my great relief there was no religion, which resulted in my becoming less aware of my deficits and gaining confidence in my abilities. The aunts would go from child to child, making sure we would not become confused or get stuck.

After about an hour and a half, we would learn new songs together to the accompaniment of a guitar, played by *Tante* Ingrid. Some afternoons we would draw or make cards and stars to send home for Christmas. We also rehearsed for our own Christmas play, and because we all had a lot of input, I could finally be a shepherd with a beard and have a small sheep made from a white pillow. I learned so much in this idyllic, happy school atmosphere, which was so unregimented and yet not at all chaotic.

I wrote letters to my mother and drew many pictures so she could see the beautiful world I was living in. Just before Christmas I got a short letter from her. She was still in the hospital and likely to remain there for some time. I was pleased to get the letter, of course, and sad that she was still sick, but I was actually relieved that I did not have to come home for some time.

I had settled in at the Kinderhaus am Hohenwald (Children's Home at the High Forest) remarkably fast and well. Maybe I had a slight attachment disorder, but I rather think that I had learned early on, through having so many unsettling experiences, to adapt to new situations, and I developed a keen sense about which environments were wholesome for my own survival. I made new friends, one of them a seven-year-old boy named Michael. We were both the skinniest kids and got weighed at least twice a week. By the end of December I had gained nearly three pounds, which on my frame was stupendous.

Inside I was experiencing a feeling of lightness, nearly emptiness, as the fear, guilt, and shame somehow moved out beyond the mountain peaks. Alas, it was only going to be a temporary reprieve.

CHAPTER 19

Our policy is directed not against
any country or doctrine but against
hunger, poverty, desperation, and chaos.
—George C. Marshall (1880–1959),
"The Marshall Plan Speech" (June 5, 1947),
Harvard University, Cambridge, Massachusetts

At the end of January, Mother's letters became more frequent, and through them I learned the reason why I was able to stay in such a magical place. It was all because of an American man named George Marshall who had had an idea for a plan to help the countries in Europe after the terrible war. He was especially concerned about the children, whom he wanted to grow up healthy and happy.

I could not comprehend why this man had chosen me out of so many thousands of children. And how did he know about me? Who else but a relative, a family member would be so generous and kind? So in my childish imagination I adopted this man with his amazing plan as my uncle. From then on, January 1951, for most of my remaining childhood and early adolescence, I included this brilliant man in my evening prayers. Kneeling at the side of my bed, I said a short prayer, blessed my immediate family, our house doctor, the Rickers, *Onkel* Bibow, and then paused, while my thoughts went to my image of America beyond the stars to the one American who was closest to my heart: "Good night, Uncle Marshall, may God protect you (*Gute Nacht, Onkel Marshall, Gott beschütze Dich*)."

I held on to the image of this man so full of goodness, decency, and compassion long after I stopped being a Catholic, holding him as a symbol of peace and love. Without knowing it, I had acquired an extraordinary "uncle" for myself, one whose career was nothing short of awe inspiring. Not only would he be given the Nobel Peace Prize in December 1953; he had been a great general and chief of staff to President Roosevelt during World War II, ambassador to China under President Truman, and secretary of state in 1947, which was when he first conceived of this very ambitious and noble plan to stop Europe from falling into chaos and to prevent the spread of communism.

"The Marshall Plan," as it became known, will always be, for Americans as well as Europeans, the greatest achievement of George Marshall. Marshall and his advisers, along with Harry Truman, the American Congress, and the American people, were givers of life and new hope for millions of Europeans. Without the European Recovery Program, many of us would not have made it. From July 1948 to June 1951, Congress appropriated thirteen billion dollars (approximately one hundred billion in today's dollars). This enormous sum helped the economically, physically, and spiritually shattered victims of war, including the children, and was administered by American and local authorities.

Thinking about it today still brings tears of gratitude to my eyes. That we could have mattered enough for people thousands of miles away to make sacrifices for us—people for whom we were just unknown faces—is miraculous. George Marshall is still one of my heroes, a visionary for peace, a humanitarian and statesman who understood what it would take to keep communism from spreading into Western Europe.

But back then, in the winter of 1950–51, I was unaware of the greatness of these men and unable to understand the incredible generosity of the American people. What I did comprehend, however, was that I was saved, first from hunger and then from my inner suffering and fears.

Now I understand that the image of George Marshall and my love and longing for all things American represented my attempt to connect with someone and something good, safe, and generous. At the same time I was trying to bury the horrendous images and events I had witnessed deep in my subconscious. But they were never eradicated, not even in my mountain paradise, as even there I would have frequent nightmares, waking up in utter terror.

During those days my attention for everything around me was sharpened. I was drawn out of myself and into the surrounding world, where the alpine environment was waiting for me to join in the dance. Those four months in the Austrian Alps started to restore and awaken my spirit and allowed me to be a real child again. Something wonderful was growing within me, often tickling me in the throat, so I had to sing or laugh to give the newborn feelings more space.

I remember that winter and early spring so vividly: my whole being hummed and vibrated in my growing body. The natural wild beauty of the mountains, the wind that made the trees sing, the majestic clouds that galloped like playful horses over the snow-covered peaks, the mountain birds, my first glimpse of a peregrine falcon, wild goats, sheep, and marmosets—I was captivated by the world around me. I felt a oneness with the earth and sky, the mountain streams, and the vast alpine pastures, as they were slowly undressed by the spring sun and the receding hands of melting snow. I, too, came out from under my cover, reclaiming my innocence! I had survived, I felt loved and a deep sense of belonging. "Oh, *Onkel* Marshall, if you could have seen me then! Thank you."

I continued to put on several more pounds as the weeks went by, did well in our "school," and learned much about the natural world, the kindness and constancy of the adults, friendship with other children, and, as there was quite a turnover, letting go and making new friends.

The days flowed harmoniously from the winter season into a lovely pre-spring, when a warm wind (*Föhn*) would blow from the south down into our valley and send long icicles, which had grown along the eaves, crashing down into the softening snow. The shoveled and trodden-down paths now revealed brown earth and rocks, and it was possible to go for long walks. Sometimes we would even go as far as Mittelberg to buy something sweet at the bakery. Or we could walk along the bottom of the valley, along the Breitach to the small village of Hirschegg, past dairy farms, visiting the cows sunbathing in the muddy farmyard. Small streams would cross our paths, and every now and then we could see little tufts of brand-new grass, with a green that foretold all the delights of the coming season.

Our boots were caked in heavy mud when we returned and had to be cleaned and rubbed with chicken fat to keep them waterproof. Then the weather would suddenly change, cold north winds blew, and everything froze again, making skiing treacherous. But when the sun was out, the thawing would continue, as did our late-morning naps in the sun. Mealtimes were always special to me, as were the games we played, our singing, learning poems, performing our own plays, and regular school time, which lasted longer as the days lengthened.

I did not want to leave this safe valley, where the blue sky looked as if it were holding everything together, the peaks, the trees, the houses, and us, creating a perfect, safe, and uncomplicated world. I missed my mother, but I did not want to leave *Onkel* Hans und *Tante* Udi. Nonetheless, I was aware that I could not stay here indefinitely and that before long I would have to leave.

After Easter I started to get anxious as the day of my departure drew near. Then one morning one of the "aunts" took me to Mittelberg and from there to Oberstdorf, outside the valley, and put my small case and me on a direct train to Stuttgart. It was a day of many tears. I remember crying quietly on the train, because leaving the mountains behind was particularly painful. They had become my friends and protectors; I knew their individual faces and shapes, and it hurt terribly to leave them not knowing if I would ever see them again.

As the train moved northwest I slowly started to get excited at the prospect of seeing Mother, Gabi, and Tina again. Outside the window the dramatic mountain terrain gave way to gentler hills, and at times the landscape appeared almost flat. There was little snow now; oxen pulled plows through the ground, and the plowed earth shone like dark metal when the sunlight hit it. The train sped over the Danube and two hours later approached Stuttgart. I could see the ruins, the dirt, and the general dreariness. I made a vow then to return soon to my beautiful mountain paradise. Anyhow, Uncle Marshall was coming with me; he lived so deep in my heart by now that I always felt his protection and caring. Whatever happened, he would take care of me. He had really become the kind of father I had longed for: a man who only wanted what was good for me.

As the train slowed, we passed by a park, gray and drab. But then I saw a yellow bush, forsythia, which had exploded into bloom, and next to it some golden daffodils announcing the end of winter and the sure coming of spring.

Mother looked much better and healthier than when I had last seen her. She was astonished at how much I had grown and was delighted at my rounded cheeks and suntan. She held me close to her for a long time. It felt good to be her little daughter again. Tina did not look good, and within a few months she was sent to visit the Stingele family at Kinderhaus am Hohenwald. For her, too, it was a great gift and helped her survive for many more years. Gabi showed little interest in anything; she was a pretty fifteen-year-old, going to the *Gymnasium* (secondary school) in the city and helping my father in his new shop, with the "infamous" Frau Roggentin. Mother and Gabi did not get on with each other. Gabi was Father's favorite and able to overlook his conduct.

But all that did not bother me as much as it had before. I had changed. There was a quiet, peaceful place in me now that was all my own.

CHAPTER 20

**From fornication and all other deadly sin;
And from all the deceits of the world,
The flesh and the devil,
Good Lord, deliver us.**

**From lightning and tempest;
From plague, pestilence and famine,
From battle and murder, and from sudden death,
Good Lord, deliver us.**

—prayer book, 1662

Back at school, things had changed. The American army trucks no longer came to bring us cooked lunches. I missed those handsome soldier friends. But we got a snack at midmorning: a warm pretzel and a small bottle of milk. I walked home for lunch, which was not too bad, as I had grown a lot of new muscles. The walk seemed easy now.

I was ahead of my classmates in all but one subject: handwriting. We had to write with pen and ink (the inkwells were built into our desks) on very rough paper. In my effort to write more neatly I pressed down too hard, which often resulted in a splattering of ink. In order to make the page look better, I transformed the inkblots into small beetles, frogs, birds, and even flowers, hoping the teacher would appreciate these whimsical illustrations to the text. But alas, this did not happen. Instead I ended up with a D in *Schönschrift* (beautiful writing, or calligraphy) next to mostly A's on my report card. But I also got another D for conduct and behavior, after a glorious A for participation. The reason given

First Communion

was that I talked a lot without first raising my hand and waiting to be called on, or I made funny remarks to cause the other students to laugh. It appeared that I had found my voice a bit too literally. This would become a habit of mine all through school, much to the distress of my mother. I was bubbling over and so glad to be alive and free, especially as our lives improved gradually and food became more plentiful.

The only thing that held my lively temperament in check was Catholicism and the idea of going to hell if I did not change my ways. But over the years that threat no longer worked either, as I made up my own image of hell. It was a pleasant place, a trifle too hot maybe, but filled with interesting people who did not conform and were original in their thinking. They were all sitting around a very hot campfire, cooking green pea soup with ham, and singing folk songs to the accompaniment of a guitar. Anything was better than becoming an angel and having to sit on a cloud by oneself for eternity singing endless hallelujahs.

It was at this time that we began to receive packages from the United States. Total strangers who had warm hearts sent these "CARE packages," Mother told us. On one such occasion, we opened a gift box that came from a town in South Dakota. A bright orange fruit rolled out. I picked it up, and the wonderful smell made me bite into it. It tasted bitter. Mother laughed: "That is an orange; you have to peel it." So we did and shared it, and I immediately knew it was the most heavenly fruit that I had ever tasted. For many years after that, I believed that South Dakota was a subtropical place. It had to be if they could grow oranges there. Years later I was shocked to learn that South Dakota was a cold and barren place in the winter and that such places could exist in the land of my saviors.

The rest of the parcel contained a pound of real coffee, two Hershey chocolate bars, dried fruit, a little picture book about a man dressed in leather wearing a raccoon hat (complete with tail) on his head, chewing gum, a few cans of real sausages, dried yellow egg powder, dried milk, pumpkin seeds, and two pairs of nylon stockings with seams for Mother's beautiful long legs. We received several of these exciting packages.

When my mother came to visit us after we had immigrated to the United States from England in 1977, she thanked everyone she met in her broken English for all the kindness they had shown Germany when the need was so great. Most people replied with a "You are welcome," which reduced Mother to tears and more thanks. She came to the States many times before her death in 1992 and saw everything through rose-colored glasses: the people were beautiful, the supermarkets like a dream, and the spaciousness of the countryside unbelievable. And all she saw was Rhode Island. What would her reaction have been to the plains of the Midwest; the Great Lakes region; the West with its mountain ranges, deserts, and the Pacific coast; and the beauty of the Everglades and subtropical Florida, where oranges do grow? She became a self-appointed goodwill ambassador for America when she went back home.

Because of my long absence I had missed classes in catechism and had to go twice a week to the parish house, next to the Catholic Church, to be instructed in private by the head priest, Dr. Hermann Breucha. This would prepare me to go to confession, followed by First Communion at the beginning of May. I remember how scared I was to sit on a hard chair and be told about all the possible sins I had already committed or might commit in the future. *Pfarrer* (Father) Breucha looked at me with his penetrating eyes as if he already knew what a miserable sinner I would become. My face burned with the heat of shame and guilt, my ears felt as if they might drop off, and I had a great desire to run out of the room, the parish house, and all the way back to my alpine refuge where I had felt whole and good.

The first Saturday in May I was finally deemed ready to go to confession. I felt naked and was convinced that God, through his servant the priest, would refuse me forgiveness and condemn me to suffer in hell for all eternity. At that time I somehow still believed in the church's interpretation of hell as a place of unimaginable physical suffering.

I stood in line that Saturday afternoon. It was a brilliant day outside, but inside the church it was dark and musty. I allowed old ladies to go ahead of me, not out of politeness, but because I could not pull enough courage out of me to enter the confessional, kneel down in front of the wooden screen, and recite my sins. Not that I had that many to confess; mostly it was stuff like forgetting my prayers, using the Lord's name in vain, having unkind thoughts, vanity, envy, and a big chunk of gluttony, in the form of thinking too much about food and when and what I would eat.

Even today I think about food quite a lot. When I am cooking and shopping, it can hardly be avoided. Whether it comes from the early years of deprivation or whether it is simply an inborn trait, the fact is, I love food. I love preparing it, eating and sharing with others, and celebrating the abundance and availability of all the wonderful food as a blessing. So maybe I was not as gluttonous as I then thought.

Finally my turn came, and I stepped inside behind the dark brown velvet curtain. I heard *Pfarrer* Breucha's voice—it was scary and comforting at the same time—and I rattled off my litany of childish transgressions. Before I knew it, I was blessed, absolved, and asked to say three Our Fathers and three Hail Marys. The relief was enormous. And just as I was about to get up from the pew, a ray of the afternoon sun struck the cross at the altar, right across Jesus' bleeding heart. I saw it as a sign that God was pleased with me after all.

I met Mother outside after the ordeal, and we went to a shop where I had my hair cut short, because I wanted to look like my new friend from school, Nicoline Post. All my curls were cut off together with the light-blonde streaks of sun-bleached hair from last summer. I could hardly look in the mirror. This will cure me of vanity, I thought. I hated the way I looked; silent tears streamed down my cheeks as this complete stranger stared back at me. The only consolation I had was that my way to hell had been postponed, at least for now, and I was allowed to march in tomorrow's procession as a child bride of Christ.

The next morning I put on my white Communion dress, which Mother had made for me. It came just above my knees and exposed the scabs I had from falling the previous week. I carried a long ivory-white candle, with a garland of fresh white daisies spiraling up, and a thick wreath of wild daisies crowned my head. My friend Nicoline wore a similar short dress, but her flowers were fresh lilies of the valley, whose scent was sweet and fragrant.

The Mass was lovely, with nice singing, but the actual Communion was a bit disappointing. I didn't know what I had expected the "Body of Christ" to taste like, but the thin wafer that was placed on my out-stretched tongue got stuck immediately onto my palate, which was very annoying. I could not taste it and had to stop myself from reaching inside my mouth to scrape it off. Also, I was extremely hungry, not having had anything to eat since the previous evening, so I started to fantasize about going back up front for another wafer. At the same time, my conscience was reminding me that all these thoughts were sinful and would have to be confessed next Saturday. It was going to be really difficult to be a good Catholic, and I could not imagine how I would ever manage to keep all the commandments. Maybe I was not cut out to be a member of this demanding faith. I should talk about this with

Herr Neuwirth and ask him about what it took to be a Protestant. Oh, no, what terrible thoughts were entering my mind.

After the service we had a nice late breakfast at home with fresh rolls, butter spread, and Mother's plum butter. *Tante* Marga came and gave me a small gold-plated watch with a black velvety wristband. From Mother I got a real fountain pen, which made writing a veritable pleasure from then on. So it turned out to be a good day. In the end I felt that God had smiled on me and that maybe I would get the hang of being a good Catholic over time. For what it was worth, I was now a real member of the Catholic Church.

From then on I went to confession every Saturday afternoon, followed by Holy Communion on Sunday morning and again on Wednesday, at 7 a.m. before school, on an empty stomach, of course. Quite often I did not last until we got back to school. Everything would suddenly go black, and I would wake up on the cold flagstones of the church floor or pass out at school during the first period. I still had to put on some more weight, and nobody suspected that I might be a bit hypoglycemic.

As the weeks progressed, I became aware that each confession was identical to the one before. I knew the list by heart. So one day I looked at my catechism book and picked something else to confess to, just for variety. As I had not killed anybody, I chose "committed adultery" and added it to my list. *Pfarrer* Breucha showed no surprise but gave me a few extra Hail Marys. Years later I discovered that he had told my mother about it and heaven knows who else. He probably dined out on this story for years. I was quite indignant and felt that he was the sinner now, as he had broken the silence of the confessor.

CHAPTER 21

Mutter tanzt, und sieht mich nicht.
Wer ist die Frau?
Sie singt, sie lacht, sie ist so jung,
Wenn sie's nicht ist
Wer bin ich dann?

Mother dances, she sees me not.
Who is this woman?
She sings, she laughs, she is so young,
If that's not her,
Then who am I?

—Sabina de Werth
(one of the author's earliest poems, 1951)

Before I went away to Austria, I had made a new friend at school. Her name was Nicoline Post, and she was assigned to sit next to me in class; we became friends almost instantly. I was immediately taken with this girl, whom I considered very exotic in her light-gray pleated flannel skirt and light-yellow twin set. She was slim like me, and her ash-blonde hair was cut short in a pageboy style. I thought she was the most special person I had ever met. We wrote letters to each other while I was in Austria, and on my return and after our First Communion we became very close friends.

Her father was in the diplomatic service, and her mother was a baroness whose family had escaped to Paris from their estates in Latvia. She was an elegant and refined lady; her dark hair parted in the middle

Frau Post with daughters, and Mother with Sabina and Tina

Nicoline, Sabina, Tina; Ree Franziska in front

and nestled in a bun above her swanlike neck. The skin of her face looked like stretched ivory silk over her high cheekbones, and she moved with such grace in her fine clothes that she appeared to be gliding. Her voice was soft, and she spoke with a lovely foreign accent. When the father was home, he conversed with his children in English, which sounded very different from the way the American soldiers had spoken.

The Posts rented a large villa on the slopes among the vineyards that led down into the city of Stuttgart. The rooms were mostly paneled in wood and had very little furniture, which made them appear huge. What furniture there was must have been French, as it was adorned with lots of gilded brass and inlay.

Once or twice a week I was allowed to go home with Nicoline after school and stay until suppertime. The terrain around her house was a children's heaven. Pergolas, statues, an overgrown labyrinth, an unused empty swimming pool, garden sheds, a gazebo—all dreadfully neglected and spooky—provided a wonderful place for us to play. Nicoline had a younger sister, Ree Franziska, and two even younger brothers, Constantin and Clemens. They were all beautiful children and great to play with. Frau Post's first name was Ree Curda, and to my great delight she and Mother met at a school function, connected instantly, and became lifelong friends. Herr Post was mostly in Bonn, the new German capital, at the *Bundestag* (parliament), presided over by Chancellor Konrad Adenauer.

Sometimes the Post children and I ventured farther down the hill toward Stuttgart. We were especially fascinated by the ruins of a once-elegant villa. This became our new favorite and secret playground. The whole plan of the first floor could be seen. Some walls were still standing, the chimney was nearly intact, and in the bathroom were a cracked toilet and the remnants of a bathtub, now filled with slimy green water and leaves. In the kitchen a few black-and-white tiles were still intact, and little yellow flowering weeds came through the grout.

We liked to play "house," which we also called "mother and father." Most of the time I took the part of the father, Nicoline was the mother, and her siblings were our children. I pretended to go to work and then come home with an armful of vegetation, old chestnuts, acorns, green weeds, wild mushrooms, and, if I could find one, a wriggling worm. Then we would all prepare a delicious pretend meal in the remnants of the kitchen. We used bricks to make a table and five seats. Nicoline had made some bread or cake with reddish earth and rainwater, decorated with pretty little yellow flowers.

After our dinner I played with "my children" or told them made-up stories about imaginary places, loosely based on my recent experiences in the Austrian Alps. It was all a lot of fun, especially as we had to keep it a secret from our parents. We were strictly forbidden to enter any ruins because of the danger of unexploded ordnance. But being young, we felt invulnerable and immortal.

One September day, just before my tenth birthday, Nicoline and I saw a black Mercedes driving down the driveway. A man stepped out and opened the door for a very elegant lady, his wife, and asked to look around. The two then entered the house. That was the moment Nicoline told me that the house was for sale and that they might be leaving soon to live in Athens, Greece. Her father had gotten a position at the German Embassy there. I could hardly take in all the news, as I was busy trying to remember where I had seen the man with the Mercedes before. His wavy hair, his pleasant voice and smile seemed so familiar. And then, just as the couple emerged from the house, it hit me.

I walked toward them, plucked up my courage, and asked: "Excuse me, but are you Wolfgang Windgassen?" He seemed pleased at being recognized: "Yes, I am. Are you interested in opera?" "Oh, no, not at all, but my big sister Gabi is. She has millions of newspaper photos on the wall next to her bed, and when you sing on the radio she gets quite hysterical if we snigger, talk, or pull faces." Herr Windgassen grinned and pulled out a postcard with his portrait on it and signed the back: "for Gabi." Then he shook my hand, asking me to give his greetings to my big sister. And with that, they drove off. I was very excited about this; now I could brag to Gabi and she would be so jealous that I had met the opera star.

Wolfgang Windgassen was at the Stuttgart State Opera and was the most famous Wagnerian tenor in Germany, maybe Europe. They called him a "*Heldentenor,*" meaning a tenor well suited to play the hero (*Held*) in Wagnerian operas because of his good looks and penetrating voice. Gabi had been taken by my father (of course!) to the opera; I think it was to hear *Siegfried*. It made such an impression on her that at age sixteen she became obsessed with the mythical German hero and turned Tina and me totally against Wagner's operas.

When I got home, I told Gabi—very slowly to maximize the dramatic effect—that I had had a very relaxed conversation with the man she loved more than anyone. And not only that, but we had shaken hands at the end. Gabi nearly lost it: "Oh, my God, which hand did he shake, was it your right?" Here she nearly pulled my arm out of the socket, staring at my hand, which had suddenly become an object of devotion. "I forbid you to wash this hand, oh, let me touch it." Finally I told her what we had talked about and pulled out the postcard with his autograph.

I don't recall exactly what she said, but I can still see the trancelike and ecstatic look on her face; she was holding her breath and then burst into tears. It all seemed extremely crazy to me. But for a few days, I was the most important person in my sister's life, her link to something bigger than all of us.

A few weeks later, school had finished early; I came home, entering through the terrace doors and stopped, totally taken aback by what was happening in front of my eyes. Loud music streamed from a gramophone, along with exotic rhythms and someone singing in a language I had never heard before. In the middle of the parquet floor Mother was dancing with a multicolored, checkered tablecloth, which she moved like a bullfighter's cape. Every now and then she joined in a refrain with the words *Bessa me, bessa me mucho* (Kiss me, kiss me again and again). She did not notice me. Her face was strangely transformed, looking more like a young girl's; her hair was down and wild; small pearls of sweat had formed on her forehead, around her nose, and upper lip.

Who was this woman, so out of control? Certainly not my mother. And then I noticed *Onkel* Bibow. He had the same expression of utter bliss and abandonment and was embracing our old black broom as a dancing partner, swaying with it to the music. These two "adults" were laughing occasionally, Mother swirling this way and that to the wonderful music that permeated everything. I drank all this in, perplexed and excited at the same time. I knew I had discovered some kind of secret, a way grown-ups were when the kids were not around.

Finally the music stopped, and Mother caught her breath and came back to earth. She brushed her hair out of her face and saw me. And in an instant her expression returned to the way it always was, a bit tired, sad, carrying a lot of responsibility. Again, she became the mother I was used to.

I can see her dancing still when I close my eyes. The encounter has become one of the most unforgettable moments of my childhood, foreshadowing what lay ahead in my own life and giving me such happiness and a treasure I can come back to again and again.

CHAPTER 22

Summer afternoon—summer afternoon;
To me those have always been
The two most beautiful words
In the English language.

—Henry James (1848–1916)

The rest of the school year I had to study very hard to get ready for the entrance exams to the *Gymnasium*. Mother decided that now was a good time to do something about my lisp, which had been cute while I was little but might be an impediment for me later on. She had found a speech therapist and had saved enough money for a few sessions. It was a long walk after school to his house. Mother left me on the doorstep, confident that I could find my way back.

I rang the doorbell, and an old, fat, and nearly bald man opened the heavy oak door. For some reason I took an immediate dislike to him. His huge nose was covered in bumps and had a bluish-red appearance, and his lips were fleshy and incredibly wrinkled. He led me into a small, nearly empty room with two chairs, positioned very close and facing each other. I had to sit on one of them, with our knees touching, leaning forward so his face was just inches from me. In that position I was asked to watch his lips and mouth while he spoke.

He began by saying "zzzzzzzzz," at the same time pulling back his monster lips and revealing hideous yellow teeth. Not only did he sound like some nasty fly, but his breath hit me with such force that I wanted to gag because it smelled so horrible. After a long time it was my turn to put my tongue on my palate, just above the inside of my upper teeth, and make sounds like an angry fly in a bottle. This went on for an eternity, after which I was made to repeat sentences in which nearly every word started with an *s*, one example was *Susie sag mal saure Sahne* (Susie just say sour cream). I could hardly wait until the hour was over, pay the man his ten marks, and get outside to breathe fresh air again.

Mother insisted I go back the following week. When the day came, I dragged my feet and was fifteen minutes late, which is very rude in a country where punctuality is nearly a religion. So I endured more *z*'s and *Susie* sentences, thinking that this torture should be added to hell's punishments.

On the way home, and for the next few days, I practiced with great concentration, so that my tongue would get used to the new position. By the end of the week my lisp was history. The "aversion therapy" had worked; I was willing to learn anything just so I would not have to go back and smell whatever was rotting in the old man's stomach. This episode did not reveal me as a compassionate person, I am ashamed to say. Mother was pleased, however, and considered it money well spent.

West Germany had gradually returned to a more normal country. We now had a new currency, the deutsch mark, and a real government in Bonn on the Rhine, with a very old but able chancellor, Konrad Adenauer. He was already seventy-three when he stepped into office in 1949.

We also had a new national flag. At school we were once given small paper flags to wave and welcome along the street the first postwar president of the new German Republic, Theodor Heuss. He looked very distinguished and had the friendliest face and warm, blue eyes. He was from Stuttgart and much beloved by all. He also was a great scholar and had been an outspoken critic of the Nazi regime, which had burned his books.

He was known for his long speeches to the indigenous Swabians, many of whom wanted to expel all refugees. But he spoke passionately about tolerance and promised that the new Germany would be a land where all Germans were welcome and where people would help those who had suffered and lost so much during the previous war. Mother nearly crept into our small radio to hear these speeches, and my admiration and fondness for this grandfatherly man came mostly through her.

We noticed relatively little of the American occupation in our daily lives. Sometimes I saw American soldiers, out of uniform, in the center of Stuttgart. They could be recognized by their height, their swagger, their crew cuts, and chewing gum. I found them fascinating. They were, after all, the "children" of Uncle Marshall, who was still keeping watch over us, making sure we were safe, healthy, and, if possible, happy.

In the summer of 1952 I was allowed to take the train on my own to visit my *Omi* (grandmother) in Eningen in the Swabian Alps, a low mountain range consisting of ancient volcanoes of exceptional beauty. *Omi* had moved back to the place where she had been born and where her half brother Hermann and some of her friends still lived. Hermann would become a major figure in my young life.

So here I was being put on the train by Mother, who, much to my embarrassment, asked an older lady in a third-class compartment to please make sure that I got off in Reutlingen, where my grandmother would be waiting for me on the platform. I felt I was old enough to travel without being chaperoned, as I had no trouble reading the names of all the stations the train passed through. It was a *Bummelzug* (a slow, rambling local train), which seemed to halt at every manure heap, but I enjoyed the thirty-five-mile ride. We passed fields that stood high with ripening wheat and rye and orchards where small green apples and pears were visible on the trees.

Omi picked me up as arranged and carried my small suitcase to the tram stop. We had to change onto another tram on a big, wide plaza with lovely timbered houses on one side, a fountain surrounded by flowers in the middle, and on the other side a big baroque church. After a few minutes we rolled out of town into open land. My heart felt light as some mountains in the distance came into view. Soon I noticed some gardens and houses, and at the next stop we got out. From there we walked a long way uphill, to a fairly new part of the village of Eningen.

Grandmother rented two rooms in the attic of a small one-and-a-half-story house, which was part of a development made up of identical houses and duplexes forming a large square. A gate led through a white picket fence into a wonderful small front garden filled with an array of flowers, mainly dahlias and gladioli in every imaginable color, as well as fragrant roses. Free-roaming chickens, a small vegetable garden, and an outhouse took up most of the backyard.

The landlady, Frau Blank, was a round, apple-cheeked woman who always wore an apron over her brightly patterned summer dresses. She looked like someone out of a fairy tale, kind and full of laughter. *Omi* lived very frugally upstairs, as she had to manage on a very meager pension and the money *Tante* Marga and Mother managed to send her. The small kitchen had a shelf next to the sink with two hotplates for cooking, a square table with two wooden chairs, and a small armchair in which *Omi* spent most of her waking hours. The only dormer window looked out over the square. To get to the bedroom, we walked along an unlit hallway past the steep staircase. *Omi* had two single beds on opposite walls and one window facing east, a chest of drawers, and an old oak wardrobe. This monstrosity often frightened me during the night with its creaking in the dark. It stood there like an evil monster against the white wall, ready to pounce on me at any moment.

On my first night I could barely sleep. The bell of the nearby church tower rang incessantly, once at a quarter past the hour, twice for half past, three times at a quarter to, and four times for the full hour, followed by the number of the hour it was. It was a cacophony right up until midnight—from 11 p.m. until 12 a.m. I heard the clanging of the bell twenty-seven times. But in time I got used to it and could sleep through.

Omi had to use the white chamber pot frequently during the night. I can still see her in her stiff white nightgown, with her gray hair braided in the back down to her hips, lowering herself onto the rim of the china pot. I heard her knees creak and swore to myself never to get that old. *Omi* was in her sixties then, at a time when women felt old, and the fact that she had not embraced a man since Grandfather's death in 1933 added to her own sense of old age. I was glad I did not have to use the pot with the painted roses on the outside very often as my young bladder had a great storage capacity. In the morning I carried *Omi's* "water" carefully down the steep steps, through the back door, past the chickens to the brick outhouse.

For breakfast I had two soft-boiled eggs with fresh orange yolks from the chickens downstairs and bread with local honey, all washed down with warm milk. I was in charge of doing all the shopping. That meant getting fresh milk in *Omi's* milk bucket, bread from the bakery, and maybe a hundred grams (three and a half ounces) of some cold cuts for supper from the butcher's shop. Shopping had to be done daily, as few people had refrigerators in those days.

I had brought my favorite doll, named Antigone after a girl at school. After breakfast I introduced her to the many chickens and the rooster, as well as the vegetable garden of peas, beans, lettuce, and big globes of creased and ridged tomatoes. Then I ventured out into the wide square where some girls were playing hopscotch. They invited me to join in, and in a few days I had many new friends and felt quite at ease.

One girl was named Ruth, and she and I liked each other immediately. She lived about five minutes down the street in a modest house. On rainy days I would go there and play board games with her. But most of the time I accompanied her as she did all the chores that were expected of her. This would take us to the center of the old village of Eningen. We'd walk by the blacksmith's shop, a carpenter whom we could watch at work through his open door, a coffin maker, and a small park on the square in front of the big church where a farmer's market took place twice a week.

Ruth had to go every day to some fields and an orchard garden to milk her family's two goats and water the two workhorses. She tried to teach me how to milk, but hard as I tried I could not master the skill. I was too afraid of hurting the udder with my squeezing. In the orchard the ripening plums were small yellow mirabelles, not much larger than a cherry, sweet and juicy; there were also red shiny plums and my favorite: small oval blue ones with yellow-green flesh, a sour skin, and a tongue-curling spicy sweetness on the inside, great for pies and flans.

A LONG SILENCE

The two horses had wonderfully hairy ankles, their straight, long, blondish hair obscuring the hooves. They were stocky and powerful, so I kept my distance. But the hay barn was nice, and we often sat on the second level, looking out, chatting, reading, and in later years talking about boys. Ruth was nearly two years older than me and knew a lot about sex from her older brother and his friends; she had also picked up the facts of life through watching animals copulate and giving birth. Much of what she told me I took with a certain skepticism; it sounded too outrageous. Ruth was only getting the basic education, no secondary school for her, and planned to leave school as soon as she was fourteen to become an apprentice at a bookkeeping firm.

As August progressed and the days turned noticeably shorter, it was time to harvest the wheat. Ruth's whole family—grandparents, aunts, and uncles—and some neighbors came out early. The women brought baskets and small sacks, while most of the men carried long-handled scythes over their shoulders; others had long-tined pitchforks. I was allowed to come along, following the singing, laughing, and chattering procession. The day promised to be dry and not too hot.

When we arrived at the large field that stretched like a tapestry uphill, the men lined up and began to march forward slowly, swinging their scythes in unison, only stopping occasionally to sharpen the blades with whetstones they carried in the pockets of their baggy trousers. The women followed, making sheaves out of the cut stalks, while Ruth and I and some other youngsters ran around and tied the sheaves into large bundles, being careful not to shake the ears of wheat too much in order not to lose the grain. It was hard work, and I was glad when the two shire horses arrived pulling a large cart with high planks on each side.

With the aid of the pitchforks, the bundles went flying in long arches onto the wagon. There was a pattern to it. The men took turns as the load grew higher, their motions nearly choreographed. Then the women laid out large canvases and brought jugs of cider, pies, cheese, and long flans topped with plums, nuts, and sugar out of their baskets.

It wasn't even noon yet, but the feast began amid laughing and joking as the alcoholic cider loosened everybody up.

All this was so fascinating to me, and I did not stop to wonder why everything was done by hand. I did not know that agriculture had been turned back forty or more years due to the lack of machinery and gasoline. Few tractors were left; everything made of metal had been confiscated for the war effort. It was as if time had been reset to capture my grandparents' experience. I feel privileged to have had a glimpse into a world that would only exist for a few more years. Harvesting was easy to understand and to take part in.

Finally, I got to ride with Ruth on top of the wagon of golden sheaves, now covered by white sheets, into the village to the threshing place. What a marvelous view we had from our perch, being taken through the village like queens entering our domain with a throng of small children far below following us. It was a world I had never known and would never see again.

The threshing would go well into the night, well beyond the time I had promised Grandmother to be back in the afternoon. I returned so very dirty and dusty that Frau Blank's husband took the garden hose and hosed me down from head to toe and threw my clothes in a tub to be washed later. I ran upstairs with two thin towels barely covering anything. That night I heard no bells, no creaking wardrobe, and no water falling into the chamber pot. I was out for the night.

CHAPTER 23

**When it's over, I want to say: all my life
I was a bride to amazement.
I was the bridegroom, taking the world into my arms.**
—Mary Oliver (1935–), "When Death Comes,"
from *New and Selected Poems* (1992)

It was during my many stays with my grandmother Magdalena that I became a beloved niece to my *Onkel* Hermann. He was the much younger half brother of *Omi*. On Sunday around noon he often paid us a visit. Up the road he came, wearing a wonderful straw hat (a boater) and a white linen summer suit with matching shoes. When he reached our house, he'd stand at the fence; wave his light cane like a baton, his hand curved over its silver knob; and sing romantic operatic arias to announce his arrival. *Omi* would go to the window gesticulating wildly to make him stop; she was so embarrassed. I looked forward to these public displays and enjoyed his singing as well as watching the neighbors' heads appear behind lace curtains, listening to this free concert of Donizetti, Rossini, Puccini, or Verdi, and a variety of operettas.

Soon *Omi* and I would emerge through the front door and proceed down the road with *Onkel* Hermann in the middle and one of us on each side hooked into his arms. I was allowed to carry his elegant walking cane. *Onkel* worked at the French garrison as a chef (Eningen was under French occupation after the war, a less friendly experience from the one we had in Stuttgart), and all sorts of wonderful food would miraculously find its way into his kitchen, including large pork roasts, rabbits, sometimes a leg of lamb, or a rump of beef. On the way down the hill,

Omi and
Onkel Hermann

total strangers who happened to be around were invited to join our small procession and come for Sunday dinner at his house.

There his sour wife, Emmy—my aunt— would glower at the motley collection of people; she didn't dare turn anyone away, but her face expressed her wish to do so. The aroma of roasting meat was intoxicating. As the guests squeezed around the long table of the dining room—some sitting on crates with pillows, some in makeshift stools, as there were not enough chairs to go around— glasses were filled with cider from a huge stone jug brought up from the cool cellar. Despite *Omi*'s protestations I was given a glass. The cider was made from last year's

Onkel Hermann, sometime before World War I

apples, and ten months of slow fermentation had converted most of the sugar into alcohol; I got a little tipsy almost instantly.

The meat came in on a platter, followed by bowls of warm German potato salad glistening with oil and much vinegar, marbled with shredded green chicory leaves. There were also several gravy boats with ladles, filled with the most delectable gravy imaginable. I can still taste it if I close my eyes. As the feast went on and the cool cider flowed, the conversation became very animated. It was all very fascinating to an eleven-year-old.

Then the plates were cleared and dessert was served in the form of a large pizza-dough flan buried under mounds of tart purple plums, sprinkled with nuts, sugar, and cinnamon. It was heaven!

Eventually most of the women went into the kitchen to clean up. Their happy chatter was like a distant humming drone. Meanwhile, *Onkel* Hermann brought out his favorite gramophone records and sang along, standing at the end of the table in blissful abandon, his body expressing every nuance of the music and lyrics and every emotion. He especially liked recordings by the tenor Richard Tauber, who had a very lyrical and buttery voice. As the gramophone played, *Onkel*'s eyes looked far away into a world where I could not follow but wished I could. When the music stopped, someone bellowed, "*Vive la France*," pulled out a packet of small cigars, and everyone laughed, while I helped myself to yet another piece of flan.

When *Omi* returned from the kitchen, it was time for me to leave the jolly party, but we were carrying bowls of leftover food for another feast the next day.

Sometimes, during the week, *Onkel* would pick me up at *Omi*'s before sunrise, carrying a knapsack and a big bucket. We walked into the center of the village where it was still eerily quiet and caught the first worker's bus into the hills. We were going to the woods to pick wild raspberries. The bus driver dropped us off at a particular spot, and suddenly we were surrounded by silence and mist. We walked on a wide path, soft and springy like a mattress, covered in pine needles and leaves. We saw some deer scurrying off through the brush, having been

Omi at the gate

Mother and Omi, 1955

warned by the screech of a jaybird that human intruders were coming.

By now the rising sun sent shafts of hazy light through the top of the trees. Mosquitoes followed us with their whining pitch and took as much blood from us as possible before retiring and escaping from the approaching heat of the day.

After much walking we came to a clearing, which was overgrown with raspberry bushes. But we had breakfast first, some raisin bread and black tea from a flask. When we were done, Onkel showed me how to tie a one-quart aluminum bucket around my waist with some string he had brought. Then I was initiated into the art of berry picking using both hands. Sometimes I would hold one branch up with one hand and let the very ripe berries that were hiding underneath fall into my other hand. The other trick was to pick with both hands independently, left and right, picking while my eyes were already on the next target. Onkel Hermann said I was a natural when I showed him the first quart of red berries, shortly after he filled his. Raspberry picking is one thing I know I am superb at, even today. No one could ever meet my yield.

As we worked, *Onkel* began to hum and then to run up and down some scales to warm his vocal chords. Before long he was ready to throw himself, full throttle, into several Neapolitan love songs, in Italian, with endless verses. Once through the song, he invited me to join in. I had a good musical ear and caught on to the melody right away and, after several repetitions, to the refrains and some phrases too. Now we were ready to sing in harmony. When I faltered he would jump into my part and after a while drop two notes again. He had a beautiful, clear, and true tenor voice and sang with infectious verve and enthusiasm. Sometimes even birds, high above us in the tops of the pines, joined in too. It was simply marvelous.

Later, in my teens, when I went to the *Gymnasium* for girls, I was always picked to sing the leading male role in our operatic productions and even took lessons for my deep alto voice. *Onkel* Hermann would have been pleased. But nothing was ever as satisfying as those lazy summer days of singing duets in the woods.

When the small bucket of berries was full, I emptied the contents carefully into the big bucket. My fingers and hands were bright red from the juice, which covered some of the scratches and reached up to my elbows. I also managed to put the ripest berries into my mouth; they tasted so sweet and tart, full of the essence of raspberry. They became my favorite fruit and still are. I have grown large patches in England and Rhode Island as an adult, and whenever I was picking by myself, using the skills I had learned so early on, the old arias would come back and I felt the spirit of *Onkel* Hermann close to me.

We did not return to Eningen until late afternoon. I took two small containers, filled to the brim, back to Grandmother. She made a wonderful preserve from it. The main part of our harvest went to the French officers' mess—for a price, of course—and probably helped to cover some of the cost (or guilt) for next Sunday's dinner.

On rainy days the two of us might be seen collecting escargot on the hillsides; to me they were just slimy snails. We each had a burlap sack in one hand, while we picked up the snails with the other, all the while trying to keep the creatures confined. They could creep up to the opening with amazing speed, contrary to their reputation. The snails were destined to appear as a delicacy on the plates of the French officers. The military paid us one deutsch mark per kilo. I always got some of the money for my efforts and would buy something sweet and sticky for myself at the village bakery. Since *Omi* was a diabetic, she couldn't have such treats. But I'd give her the rest of the money, as I was sure that her budget was strained because of having to feed me.

An especially memorable occasion with my *Onkel* was a "business venture" during one Easter vacation. On Easter Sunday we arose early and went stalking through the dewy slopes in search of wild spring flowers. The aim was to create fresh spring bouquets to sell on Easter. First we picked yellow primroses (*primulas*) and grape hyacinths of the deepest blue, which we threw over our shoulders into the baskets we carried on our backs. When we had gathered enough, we sat down on some rocks and made small bunches. We put the fragrant pale-yellow primroses in the middle and the sky-blue hyacinths in a circle around the outside so they looked like sentinels in blue uniforms. We ended up with over fifty bouquets.

Next we rushed to the main church, arriving just as the congregation emerged into the spring sun from Easter service. We were waiting for them as they came down the steps in their holiday finery. Despite the deprivations of the postwar environment, the women were decked out in pastel-colored dresses and hats with bows and flowers, and the men wore their best, if worn, suits, hats, and colorful ties. As they filed out of the church, I held out several bunches of nature's treasure, enchanting the churchgoers both with the flowers and my performance as a young Eliza Doolittle. They must have felt generous after celebrating the resurrection of Christ and now the resurrection of nature. Before long we had sold all the bouquets, and my pockets were tinkling with fifty-pfennig pieces. I had completely forgotten that I should have been in church instead of having so much fun being an entrepreneur.

Being with *Onkel* Hermann was always a wonderful experience for me. He treated me with so much respect, as if I were his equal. He taught me how to observe the small things in nature, like beetles, grasses, and flowers. He told me funny stories, helped me identify the different bird songs, and encouraged me to sing. I loved him very much, as an uncle, older brother, and as my best friend. And best of all, I felt loved by him. He made me feel worthy and interesting, and he gave me the gift of belonging to the world. In his presence I could forget about my shame and never felt like a refugee.

Sometimes Mother came for a weekend. She loved *Onkel* Hermann too. She often said: "He is so kind; his heart is so big, he'd give his last shirt to a stranger." Little did we know that this would be exactly how his life would end.

In my later teens I stopped coming to Eningen, after *Omi* had to go into a nursing home. I did not see *Onkel* Hermann again or hear much of him until Mother sent me a newspaper clipping in 1961 from the *Reutlinger Zeitung* (the local newspaper) describing how he had died. I was at the University of Freiburg at the time. Years later I reconstructed his last day on earth from bits and pieces I learned from my mother and *Tante* Marga. This reconstruction follows in the next chapter. Parts of it came to me as if from a dream, in that place between sleep and wakefulness. It is meant as a tribute to a wonderful human being who deserves to be honored. He gave me so much by acting as a mentor, father, and dear friend at a time when I really needed such a person. All his life he must have lived in fear of being found out that he was gay.

CHAPTER 24

Der Lindenbaum

Am Brunnen vor dem Tore
Da steht ein Lindenbaum;
Ich träumt in seinem Schatten
So manchen süssen Traum.

Linden Trees

By the well before the gate,
there stands a lime-tree;
In its shade I dreamed
many a sweet dream.

—Wilhelm Müller (1794–1827),
set to music by Franz Schubert,
Song Cycle *Die Winterreise* (*Winter's Journey*)

From what I could piece together, *Onkel* Hermann had been accused of making sexual advances to a young man in the bathroom of a bar in Reutlingen. He was to appear in front of a judge that fateful Thursday morning in late spring. In Germany during the early 1960s, homosexuality was still considered a crime punishable by imprisonment, which was a great improvement over the torture, mutilation, and extermination imposed by the Nazi regime.

That *Onkel* Hermann had been gay came as a surprise to me. I knew nothing about such things. My mother, I found out, had known all along, and my grandmother, his half sister, suspected it and felt ashamed. It had all been cloaked in silence.

Tante Emmy, Hermann's wife, must have known. Her disappointment and disgust had frozen her face into a perpetual scowl; the corners of her mouth were pulled down in deep ruts all the way to her jawbone, telling of her suffering and unmentionable outrage. As a child I could not interpret any of this, of course, and now I feel bad that I disliked her so much.

What must it have been like on that morning, when Hermann had to get ready for court? Was he perplexed to find himself in such a humiliating position, or maybe relieved that the truth about his "affliction" would finally be revealed and he could take his punishment? Anyhow, it had come to this, and now his life was ruined forever.

It had really started after the Great War, when Hermann had gotten a job as a chauffeur for a local mill owner, Herr Müller. At the time, Hermann's father was dying from syphilis he had brought back from Flanders, and he could no longer provide for Hermann's mother and smaller siblings. Herr Müller's attention to him was both flattering and a comfort for the loss of his father. The extra cash, the few presents, shirts and jackets, even the odd touching were welcome, and the first fleeting kiss did not alert him that maybe something might be asked of him in return. One day Herr Müller had Hermann drive to the outskirts of town and there seduced him. Hermann was too confused and scared to do anything. He did not want to anger the boss, who had been so kind to him. So he went along and let himself be fondled until he climaxed. He told my mother in 1950 that after the incident he tried to hang himself, so great was his shame.

He married Emmy and had two sons, who never amounted to much. Erich, the oldest, became a drunk and a gambler. I remember him vaguely, a man with protruding large yellow teeth like a horse's and yellow fingertips from chain smoking. He always wore a brown suit, stained and shiny on the sleeves and collar from constant wear, and he reeked of stale beer, sweat, and cigarettes. Walter, the other son, looked quite presentable and had many women friends. However, as I recall, he did a stretch in prison for breaking and entering.

I imagine *Onkel* Hermann early that morning, still in bed, reluctant to face the day. I hope he had time to remember the one time in his life when he had felt truly happy, loved, and unsullied.

It was during the Second World War, somewhere in Poland. He, a mere corporal, was left with Philip, a lieutenant in charge of a nearly burned-out village, bereft of any survivors. Philip came from an upper-middle-class background. He was the exact opposite of Hermann, blond, tall, and athletic. They were both in their early forties and felt at ease with each other. Hermann would get up in the morning and hunt for some fresh eggs from the few chickens that had survived the destruction. The two grown men swam naked in the village pond, wrestled in the grass like young boys, and later made love under the blooming linden trees. They were able to push away the horrors and gruesomeness they had experienced over the last year.

Hermann lay in bed, eyes closed. He could smell the air, sweet and fragrant from the small yellow-white clusters of blossoms that covered the ghastly stench from the burned village and its inhabitants, human and animal. Just their little farmhouse had escaped the flames and explosions, and it stood as a proud reminder of good times in the charred surroundings.

"Oh, how we loved each other," Hermann might have thought. "Oh, Philip, if you could see me now."

Images of Philip floated across the inside of his eyelids. Once they had played hide-and-seek, and after a long search, which heightened his desire, he sensed and then saw the outline of Philip against the brick wall in the cellar. When he got used to the half light, he saw Philip was smiling, saw his hairless chest inside the open shirt, could anticipate the silkiness of his nearly flawless skin. When they touched, he nearly climaxed, so intense was his want. They made love, fast and nearly violently. They did not talk. It had been the most perfect moment in Hermann's entire life, and he was momentarily paralyzed by the sheer memory of it. He remembered that after their lovemaking they ran out into the glaring afternoon and into the pond to cool down. The rest of the day they slept close together under the linden trees.

In the evening they talked tentatively about the future.

Hermann asked Philip: "What are we going to do when this god-awful war is over? Where can we go? I want to be with you always." He recalled Philip's smile, a knowing sort of smile that required no answer.

And then, the next morning, some German tanks came through and picked them up. Two days later they had to rejoin their respective units. They would never see each other again.

Perhaps all this went through Hermann's head and heart that morning until a shrill shout from Emmy downstairs jerked him back to the present. Her voice had a hateful and threatening quality, and he obeyed, believing he did not deserve any better, not now. He went to the bathroom, shaved, and dug out his Sunday suit. He had to make a good impression in front of the judge.

When he came downstairs, Emmy was scrubbing pots at the sink in her old, greasy, floral-patterned housecoat, which was like a tattered cocoon in which she practically lived. In this housecoat she often sat as if imprisoned in an overstuffed sofa with half the stuffing bulging out. There was no hope that she could ever metamorphose like a butterfly into something feminine. She had obviously given up a long time ago.

Hermann was just glad she was not saying anything and ignored her killer looks. "Does she know? Has she known all these years?" He asked her to help him find his small dark-brown cardboard suitcase, the one embossed with crocodile skin patterns. She started to argue, and he eventually found it himself. No time for tea and bread. He ran out the side door to the small shed, where he put a long rope into the case.

I do not know what went through his mind just then, but I see him rushing to the tram stop. There were a few people waiting, and soon the tram to Reutlingen rolled in. He congratulated himself for thinking of the case. Everyone would think he was going on a trip, not to his own funeral. He smiled at his humor. He might get ten years behind bars, which he would never survive.

At the courthouse the doors were still locked. He looked across the street and saw the entrance to a park. Something called him there. Through the trees he could see a pinkish light reflected in a pond. Memories were flooding him again—he smelled something so familiar, so sweet, like in the half dream from early that morning. Of course, it was the linden trees and their blossoms. Reality lost its margins as he entered into a fuzzy, undefined weightlessness of some former world he had once known so many springs ago. He felt strangely tired all of a sudden; his whole skeleton and muscles wanted to let go. The ground beneath him beckoned like a downy bed. He barely made it beyond two lilac bushes, out of sight, before he sank into an earthy bed. Everything will turn out all right, he told himself. Philip will come and find me in a minute. The anticipation of their imminent reunion spread over him like a comforting blanket.

Emmy did not find out what had happened to her husband until the following day, when the police came to her house. Hermann had never shown up at court, which didn't really matter, as the charges had been dropped at the last minute. The keeper of the small municipal park had stumbled over a heap of neatly folded clothes, with a pair of black shoes beside it, right at the edge of the small artificial lake. When he looked around he saw something sticking out near the middle. He waded out toward it and saw that it was a pair of naked human feet above the surface of the water.

The police pulled out a man, in his sixties, wearing nothing but his underpants. Around his neck was a thick rope attached to a small brown suitcase filled with several of the large ornamental rocks from the water's edge. The man had obviously drowned himself, according to the coroner's report, between 10:00 p.m. and midnight the previous evening, in three and a half feet of water.

Sometimes I think of my uncle as an overflowing fountain. This wonderful, generous person, who despite having so little, felt such enormous joy in small things, and he gave more to others than he himself could hold. I see him in my dreams, in the last few minutes of his life.

A LONG SILENCE

It is always the same. It starts with the image of him undressing at the lake in darkness. He stands in his shirttails, shivering slightly; opens the buttons, one by one; slips his shirt off his shoulders and neatly folds it on the ground, the way shopgirls fold them in men's clothing stores. Only his undershirt is now left; he quickly pulls it over his head to join the other pieces on the ground, followed by his black shoes and socks.

Without looking around him, he purposefully walks with his now-heavy suitcase out into the shallow pond. The bottom is muddy and slimy between his toes, and he nearly loses his balance twice. When the water reaches his slender hips, he lifts the case up, slips the loop of the rope over his head, then continues walking. The case is pulling below his knees and makes walking difficult. The water is up to his waist. He throws himself forward, facedown. He is under the surface now, losing his sense of sight and sound, breathing in water. A short struggle, his heels break the surface of the water, kicking frantically for a moment. Then nothing, only the ever-widening circles of the rippling water, reaching the shoreline at last.

CHAPTER 25

**And he went back through the Wet Wild Woods
Waving his wild tail and walking
By his wild lone.
But he never told anybody.**

—Rudyard Kipling (1865–1936),
"The Cat That Walked by Himself,"
from *Just So Stories* (1902)

At the end of October, school always closed for a week during the final harvest time. I vividly remember our autumn vacation in 1951 because it had such a lasting effect on my sister Tina and me.

The harvest had been good, and food was more plentiful. It seemed as if summer had made a comeback, and we enjoyed short but unusually warm and sunny days, called *Altweiber Sommer* (old wives' summer), as Indian summer is called in Germany. My sister Tina and I, together with Eva and some other friends who lived on Silberpappelweg, met most days after lunch and spent most of the afternoon at the edge of the small forest. It was beautiful that time of year, even though most of the oaks and beech trees had lost their foliage. Now the forest floor was covered with a thick layer of cinnamon-colored leaves on which we could tumble. We buried each other in the dry leaves and shrieked with the pure joy of it, or we played long games of hide-and-seek. The days seemed endless, the way only children can experience time. I felt truly happy, especially as Tina came more to life with our carefree playing.

The air stayed soft and balmy for several days, the apples we stole from a nearby orchard were the sweetest and juiciest I had ever eaten, and I even forgot about sin and the damnation that would await me in hell for stealing. Life was good; I had just gotten a new bed a few days before, an early Christmas present.

The last weekday of that memorable vacation promised to be even better than the previous ones, and there was nothing that might have warned me of what was about to happen.

Tina woke me on that morning by tickling my cheek. I loved being touched and tickled; in fact, I often would give her my small weekly allowance of twenty pfennigs for half an hour's worth of soft tickling up and down my arms. She had wonderfully sensitive fingertips, and though I was really awake, I pretended to be asleep so she would continue a little while longer. Finally I had to open my eyes. Tina's face was close to mine, whispering: "Let's get up and spend all day in the forest, just you and me. We can take some larded bread with us and a bottle of water."

I was fully awake in an instant. I loved my sister very much and was excited that she wanted to spend the whole day just with me. I felt ready for any adventure with her. We jumped out of bed, threw on our clothes, and hurried into our makeshift kitchen. Mother was already up. She was never talkative first thing in the morning, but she smiled at us and cooked us a bowl of porridge each. We gulped it down.

"You two seem to be in a hurry this morning," she remarked. "I hope you won't run off all day, because I need you to help me clean the house and hang out the laundry. Grandmother is arriving on Tuesday to stay with us for a while. I want everything to be spotless; you know what a fusspot she is."

Tina used her most persuasive voice: "*Mutti*, please, today is our last real vacation day before the weekend. Please, we will help you the entire day tomorrow; I will sweep the terrace and polish the floors and whatever else needs doing."

Tina was Mother's favorite daughter (or so I believed then), and I watched her make her most irresistible face at Mother. She sat there so seriously, with her forehead pulled up slightly making two shallow wrinkles, and pleaded in her faded-blue orphan Annie's dress (handed down from Gabi), while her brown pigtails fell down over her skinny shoulders and her dark brown eyes focused with such intent on Mother. And sure enough, Mother succumbed, rather willingly, I thought. Her face lit up with a smile, and she said: "All right, then, but I shall depend on you two tomorrow."

Tina and I had won. Well, I had done nothing, really, but just keeping quiet and scraping the last of the porridge from the edges of the bowl had been enough. We washed our bowls at the sink and made two large sandwiches from dark rye bread, spread lard on it, sprinkled salt all over, and filled an old glass bottle with water.

Mother wanted to know where we were going. "Oh, just to the edge of the forest as we always do, to play and lie in the leaves in the sun and talk," Tina assured her. "We will be back before it is dark." We both gave Mother a hug and rushed outside. Tina was carrying a small knapsack with our provisions.

None of our friends were outside yet as we walked down the street. A slight mist hung over everything, and the air smelled sweet and damp. The sun announced its presence by lighting up an area of the misty sky and promised to break through any moment.

I got out of breath trying to keep up with Tina. Why was she in such a hurry? As we neared the entrance to the woods, she started to talk: "I have decided to go deep into the forest, to the place we are not allowed to go, because lovers hang out there. And you are not allowed to say where we went when we get back, all right?"

I promised, prepared to follow her to the ends of the earth. Her excitement gave me energy, and my steps became longer. I felt like a character in a fairy tale, like Hansel or Gretel. Were we going to meet a witch or some giant or something I could not even imagine?

At first we passed trees and bushes where we had ventured before, but then the path became narrow and partly hidden by the leaf cover, and it took all our concentration to follow it. I looked back, but the path had curved, and all I could see were trees. It was very quiet; the only sound came from our muted footsteps on the damp ground. Sometimes a few belated leaves sailed down from above, past us, in slow motion, as if undecided where to settle.

We entered a small clearing. Tina stopped and pointed ahead. Several rabbits were ahead of us, feeding. They froze and stared at us, their long ears erect. Then they suddenly fled together, as if by prior agreement.

The sun had broken through by now. "Let's stop and eat something," my sister suggested. We had been walking for a long time, and the bread tasted wonderful. I wanted to eat all of mine, but Tina stopped me: "We must keep some for emergencies, in case we get lost or something." She said this so calmly, as if she was already resigned to something happening. I looked at her and noticed a strange expression on her face, and I started to feel slightly frightened.

"Maybe we should turn back," I ventured, but she interrupted me sharply.

"Oh, no, I should have known that you are a scaredy-cat, and gone on my own."

"Oh, please Tina, I like coming with you and I am not scared, really I am not," I lied, as much to convince myself as her.

We continued our trek silently. The forest got very dense and was mostly firs now. I could smell the sickly odor of decaying fungi, mixed with already-rotting leaves, for here it was damp and quite gloomy. Walking behind Tina, putting my feet into the depressions her feet had just made, created a calming and almost hypnotic effect on me. We walked and walked. I was getting awfully tired but did not dare to say anything.

Suddenly Tina stopped: "I think we are here." I did not understand, here *where*? How could she know she had arrived when she had never been in this spot before? But I knew better than to ask her. She stood there several minutes with a faraway look, and I understood that I could not reach her. Her eyes were wide open, and she was watching something I could not see. All I saw was trees, the same forest floor deeply covered in leaves and needles, and a faint afternoon sun sending some light through the branches.

My eyes returned to my sister. She was motionless, listening inward. Suddenly she began to move toward a small pile of leaves to the left of us. "That's it, yes, that's it, that's where it happened." Her voice was almost inaudible and very shaky. I started to get a tight feeling in my stomach like the time a neighbor's small gray dog was run over by a car, right in front of my eyes.

"Yes, that's it, that's it," she kept repeating like a mantra, while kneeling down beside the mound. Now I was terrified and too frightened to do anything, like the time when the Russians came into our bedroom. I watched Tina moving the leaves aside, first with her hands, then with her arms, and finally she leaned into the heap and dug into it like an animal. I did not breathe and I don't think she did either; the only sound was the rustling of the leaves. And then she stopped, and I heard an awful gasping sound coming from my sister's body, as if all air and life were rushing out of her.

I moved closer, and it took a few seconds for my brain to accept what I was seeing. Close to Tina's lap lay a head, a human head, or what was left of it, with matted hair; gaping holes in the face where eyes, nose, and mouth should have been; and the whole awful mess was moving with maggots and snails. I stared at it for what seemed an eternity, and then the stench hit me with such force that I had to turn around to wretch. There is no way to describe that abominable smell.

My instinct now was to get away from this evil place. I pulled Tina's limp body away; she was sobbing quietly. I dragged her with all my might over the slippery ground, slowly at first, then faster, trying to put as much distance between the horror she had uncovered and ourselves.

I do not remember how far I pulled her and how I found the strength to do it. Finally I had to stop and catch my breath, crouching next to Tina. I brushed the leaves and dirt off her, hugged and kissed her: "I am going to get you out of here, don't worry, we are going to get out of here." I got her onto her feet; her face looked gray and her eyes dead, and I was more scared than ever before.

How long it took us to get out of the forest and how I found my way back onto our street I do not know. I held Tina's hand in mine, and we walked in a dreamlike state until it felt as if this was all happening to someone else.

Shortly before we reached our house, I started to think more clearly. Someone had to be told about what we had discovered. I did not want Tina to be questioned by the police, so I decided to go to the station alone after I had dropped her off at our terrace door, with instructions to clean herself and go to bed. The police station was only a few blocks away. I remember little about giving my account of our gruesome discovery.

The next morning the daily newspaper had this headline: "Children Discover Decapitated Corpse in Local Wood." And a day later the front page read "Four More Mutilated Women Found." Tina was in bed with a fever. I was not allowed to talk with her, but when Mother was out fetching *Omi* from the railway station, I sneaked in.

Tina told me then, in fits and starts, how she had dreamed about a man taking women into the woods, how he raped and then killed them with an ax. She said she had had these dreams over a period of two or three weeks. "Oh, if only I had done something or gone to the police," she sobbed, "maybe I could have stopped him. But you see, I thought they were only horrible nightmares, like so many I have, and that no one would believe me anyway. That's why I had to make sure." And with that she pressed her face into the pillow and wept. I held her for a while. I felt so helpless and half sick myself, trying to forget the whole thing, despite the awful flashbacks that tortured my mind.

Mother forbade us to talk about it, though today we know that this is the worst strategy for people suffering from post-traumatic stress.

Tina never fully recovered from the ordeal. I think she somehow felt responsible for the awful murders. We never mentioned them again, and for a while we were strictly forbidden to play near or in the forest. Later in life Tina often had premonitions of accidents and disasters, or thought she did. These so-called premonitions must have been a heavy burden to bear.

After a few weeks had passed, Mother took her to see a psychiatrist, because her nightmares were terrible and she was afraid to go to sleep. Once I came with them and met the doctor. I asked him point-blank how he could help my sister. He didn't really answer my question but explained to me how the psyche, the soul, can be hurt as much or even more than the body and needs time and understanding to heal. This made a great impression on me, and from that moment on I decided I would become such a "doctor for the soul," or psychotherapist, as we would say today. Sure enough, in 1960 I entered Freiburg University to study psychology to learn how to alleviate the invisible mental anguish so many people suffer from.

Just after Christmas it was Tina's turn to be sent to the Stingele family at Kinderhaus am Hohenwald. She, too, bonded with them and the magic of the place, and after her return was also homesick for the valley, right up into her adulthood. She appeared improved on her return, but a shroud of melancholy always enveloped her, no matter what.

CHAPTER 26

I couldn't help it.
I can resist everything,
Except temptation.

—Oscar Wilde (1854–1900),
from *The Importance of Being Earnest*

In the late spring of 1952, I took and passed the entrance examination to the all-girls *Gymnasium*. The first two years took place in a lovely, low building in Degerloch, with a real garden behind it and benches to sit on. This meant we did not have to walk or take the tram down into Stuttgart, as Tina had to do. She did not enjoy going to school and made no real friends.

For me, it was the exact opposite. I had inherited an outgoing personality, made friends easily, and was liked by most of my teachers and other adults. I loved the new school, which was close enough that I could walk home for lunch in just five minutes along tree-lined streets. Learning to play the recorder and being allowed to paint and sing were great, but best of all to me was that we started to learn English, the language Uncle Marshall spoke. I took to it right away and practiced all the time at home, chewing gum from the CARE package sent to us from South Dakota. It had lost its flavor long ago, but I had stuck it to my bedpost and it lasted for months, not any worse for having collected some dust.

I had also started to listen to the American Forces Network on our little radio whenever I could. I remember the Southern drawl of many of the announcers and some of the pop music. Every now and then I would understand a few words. As time went on and my vocabulary grew, I comprehended more and more, and by the time I was fourteen I had acquired an odd mixture of American accents mixed with my German one, to the surprise and often annoyance of my English teachers, who wanted us to speak "proper" English.

Despite all the improvements in our lives and my lively spirit, my body let me down frequently. I was sick a lot, with influenza, bronchitis, pleurisy, and all sorts of stomach viruses. My immune system was so weak that the next time our class had to go to the public health department to be measured, weighed, and examined, I was found wanting in all aspects. As a result, my name was put on a list so I could be sent away again (!) to the Kinderhaus am Hohenwald in my beloved valley. Uncle Marshall had done it again; he was obviously still looking out for me.

In mid-December of that year, Father suddenly reappeared, accompanied by our priest, *Pfarrer* Breucha. Father asked forgiveness and wanted to come back to us again. He promised to turn over a new leaf and be a loyal husband and father. Mother was in shock, but the good priest talked to her about the sacrament of marriage and how Jesus forgives us our sins. Well, the result was that Mother fell for it and agreed. Maybe she really hoped that her Bernd had changed and we would now have a fully functioning family. I did not trust this turnaround. Things had been so much happier and stable since he had left home. I was sure that things had not worked out with the awful Frau Roggentin and he needed someone to run his shop. Tina agreed. Later it came out that our suspicions were correct.

So Mother started to take two trams to get to the shop in Bad Cannstatt, across the river Neckar from Stuttgart, where she waited on customers, restocked the shelves, and kept the books. I think at the beginning she liked having something useful to do, and with her charm she was great with the customers. But she spent three hours a day on the roundtrip and arrived home very tired. Father usually stayed overnight at the shop during the week, sleeping in back on an old sofa. But Tina and I were convinced that he was seeing other women just as before.

Our lives changed a lot from then on. Without Mother at home during the day, we had to do everything ourselves. I really missed her. It had been so nice to come home for lunch and eat with her and talk. Now I had to fix something for myself, warm up leftover spaghetti, or eat some bread. With no one there, it all felt sad. Tina could not come home during lunch, and Gabi was now going to a trade school, learning to be a doctor's assistant. We all had to do a lot of chores, such as shopping, making beds, general cleaning, peeling potatoes, or preparing food for an evening meal.

Once Mother and Father went away for a few days to visit some factories to look at new merchandise for the shop. Gabi was put in charge to see that we all helped with the chores. She decided this meant that she would just supervise and give orders while Tina and I did all the work. She just sat on the couch and read magazines, watching me with one eye while I polished the parquet floor on my knees. If we complained, she would make threats and even hit us.

She told us we had to clean the basement and then got increasingly annoyed because we gave her lip. Suddenly she grabbed a thick rubber hose with a brass fitting at the end and began beating us with it in a blind rage. I protected my head but got several lashes on my shoulder blades and started to bleed before I managed to escape upstairs. That was it; I had had enough of Gabi's terrible anger, which she vented on our frail bodies. She threatened that if we said anything to our parents, she would hit us worse next time. I was truly frightened.

The next day after I came back from school, I knew what I had to do. I packed my featherbed, pillow, and thick overcoat in our wooden cart, with the intent of leaving home. I also took along a loaf of bread from the kitchen together with a sharp bread knife, both for cutting the bread and for protection, as well as my old chewing gum for comfort. I was never coming back. Pulling my earthly goods behind me, I passed Eva's house and soon entered the forest. I walked as quickly as I could, but pulling the cart over the exposed tree roots was difficult and I broke into a sweat. Deeper and deeper I marched into the unknown, slightly fearful but determined, thinking that if I walked long enough I might eventually get to another country and even to America. I had learned by now that America was on the planet I lived on, although the idea of it being close to the stars and the moon was hard to let go of entirely.

The forest was not as vast as I had hoped, and after a couple of hours I came onto a narrow, paved road. This I followed, and by the time it started to get dark I passed some houses. One house had no fence around it, so I sneaked behind it and hid next to an old garden shed. By now I was a bit scared but still determined to seek freedom from the oppression of my big sister. I felt a bit like the character in a book I had been reading, which dealt with oppression and revolt.

I cut a wedge of bread from the loaf, drank some water from a garden hose nearby, put on my overcoat, and squeezed into the cart, knees pulled up to my chin. The night was cool, but at least it was not raining.

I must have slept quite deeply, because it was light when I felt a tug at my arm. The owner of the house had come out early to check on his vegetable garden and found an unexpected addition to his crop. I did not want to give my name and address, so he gently led me into the house, where his wife gave me *Milchkaffee* (hot milk with a dash of coffee) and a bun. After a while I thawed out and spilled my problems, and I was persuaded to return home. My mother would be terribly upset to lose me, they said. One of their neighbors with a truck lifted my cart onto the back and me into the cab, then delivered me back home, no worse for wear.

Mother had come back unexpectedly the night before, was beside herself, and had notified the police. She was glad to have me back but mad at the same time for giving her such a fright. But when Tina and I told her what had happened, she directed her anger at Gabi. From then on Gabi never touched either one of us.

Today I feel compassion for her. She had so many responsibilities being the oldest child, and no one to help her cope with the terrible trauma of the multiple rapes. My God, she was nine and a half years old at the time! To this day she glosses over all the bad times and says she can't remember much. Oh Gabi, if only someone had been able to help you unfreeze from inside.

Meanwhile, my Aunt Marga was urged by Mother to have her teeth checked by one of our neighbors, a very successful dentist whose beautiful wife had recently left him for another man. Mother had a feeling that the two might be quite suited for each other. *Tante* Marga was widowed and felt a bit lonely without a man. Well, Mother's intuition proved correct. The good doctor fell for the attractive Marga, with her big eyes, ample bosom, slim waist, and long legs. There was a long courtship, culminating in marriage in 1953.

Now I had acquired yet another uncle, *Onkel* Otto. He and Marga had a fifty-year-old marriage together until Marga died in 2003. *Onkel* Otto turned out to be a very generous uncle to us, and he gave us all free dental service. But he was so generous in other ways, helping out financially when there was a real need. With the giving, however, came some advice and criticism as to how to spend the money or how Mother could be a better parent. He could be very opinionated and prejudiced.

After my aunt's death, I developed a very warm relationship with him. When I visit him in Stuttgart, we sit together, and he has learned to share his feelings with me. This has produced a real love and bond between us.

In his lighter moods we laugh, and he sings to me ballads from his youth, when he was a member of a fraternity in medical school in Tübingen. The songs are often quite romantic; they talk of love between young students and pretty damsels. He holds my hands as he sings, while his eyes see a world far away and long gone, a world I can only imagine.

CHAPTER 27

For the drop of water
Joy is,
Entering the river

—Chinese proverb

The year 1953 was very eventful. In the winter I bought myself my first ice skates with *Onkel* Otto's Christmas money. The local tennis club converted its big tennis courts into a skating heaven. They lined the courts with wooden boards and connectors, and sprayed the enclosed areas with water every night until there was a thick layer of ice. For a mere twenty pfennigs I could skate in the afternoon and all day on weekends. A few wooden huts were erected with a hot wood-stove inside and benches where we could sit and warm our cold feet and hands. Music flowed down on us out of loudspeakers tied to the lamp-posts; at first we heard mostly Viennese waltzes, but in later years more pop music from America was played. I remember hearing my first rock 'n' roll song and skating to Elvis Presley's "Love Me Tender."

In early spring (March 5, to be precise), I came home from school and, to my surprise, Mother was already there. She sat at the table, with her head in her hands and the radio on, and said over and over again: "*Ach Gott sei Dank, Gott sei Dank*" (Thanks be to God). When she noticed me, she explained breathlessly in between tears: "Stalin is dead, the monster is dead, and he can't hurt us anymore." I knew who Stalin was and wondered why she wasn't jumping up and down for joy, like little Red Riding Hood after the wolf had died. But I felt Mother's immense relief and somehow understood how much fear she had endured in thinking that the angry Russian hordes might return one day.

"Liegehalle" (the shed beyond the house)

Children playing outside after the snow had melted

My response was to run out into Silberpappelweg and tell everyone who was passing about the good news. Some elderly lady scolded me for being happy about the death of a human being; apparently it was not very Christian. But in my heart I could not regret the demise of a man who had been responsible for so much death and suffering. According to recent estimates, at least twenty million people died as a direct result of his brutal regime; many were executed, while others were persecuted or worked to death in the infamous Gulags. (See Robert Conquest, *Stalin: Breaker of Nations* [New York: Penguin, 1992].)

Ten days after this, I was on a train to Oberstdorf, back to the mountains for a six-week stay with the Stingele family. *Onkel* Hans and *Tante* Udi met my train, as they had some business to attend to in town, so we took the bus to Mittelberg together. Everything was the way I remembered it. I recognized the differently shaped mountains like old friends, the "Bear," the "Ram," the "*Hammerspitze*" (hammer point), but most of all the incredibly blue dome of sky above. The sun was strong and the icicles hanging on the eaves of the wooden houses were sparkling and dripping onto the street. Big slabs of snow slid down on south-facing roofs, making high piles of snow one had to maneuver around. I was treated to my first French onion soup and cheesecake for lunch at a restaurant, where a big log fire burned and illuminated our faces.

At eleven and a half years of age, my experience of being at the Kinderhaus was very different. I felt less carefree and was unable to forget my life at home as easily as the time before. Maybe I was starting to become a person and felt I needed more privacy and time alone to think. I no longer ran around naked from bedroom to bathroom, and I became increasingly aware that I was a girl, like it or not.

I had always hoped that through some miracle I would wake up one day and be a boy. I did not look forward to becoming a woman. Men were strong and powerful and could defend themselves; women were weak and seemed to have to suffer a lot and were at the mercy of men. To me the tiny swellings around my nipples were bad news.

Three years later I started to smoke cigarettes—secretly, of course—because they made me feel like one of the heroes I saw in American movies, westerns mostly, and gave me a sense of being untouchable. How wrong and foolish that turned out to be.

I started to write small poems with illustrations and doodles, most of which were not very good. I wrote many letters to Mother, Eva, and Nicoline, and found great joy in describing the natural world as I saw it. I discovered nature as a metaphor for human life—a rather egocentric viewpoint. But it helped me to put my own individual experience in perspective by viewing it in the context of the surrounding natural world, with its grand vistas and timeless qualities. It has given me a feeling of belonging throughout my life, and I have used it to cope when bad things happen.

Some of the older girls and I were allowed to take walks by ourselves. When the weather was warm, we often sat on an outcrop of lichen-covered granite rocks under a lone birch tree, still bare, and just talked and laughed the way young girls do. The snow was retreating to the higher elevations, and we took long hikes into the valley.

Our walks took us through marshes where egg yolk–colored marigolds, with their tight globelike buds and lotus-shaped open flowers, all on one stem, competed for beauty with early deep-blue forget-me-nots and a few clumps of fragrant violets. I can still hear the sound of the little streams that appeared everywhere, carrying the water from the melted snow down the slopes until it could join the Breitach, which by now was a thunderous, whitewater river. Its waters nearly reached the primitive, dilapidated covered bridge, so crossing it was scary, especially as there were big gaps between the planks, exposing the relentless torrents of roiling, icy water.

During my stay, maybe it was over Easter, the oldest of the Stingele's sons, Volkart, came home for a visit from medical school. His face had a captivating smile and his head was covered with tight dark-blond curls. He remembered me and joked around a lot, and after a day or so I could think of nothing else but him. At my age I was no longer just reading fairy tales but stories about the lives and loves of real people, such as Pocahontas, and historical kings, princesses, and heroines. From this reading, I had developed my own notions of romantic love.

One night, when I was not quick enough to go upstairs to bed, Volkart picked me up and carried me piggyback to my bed. On the way, with my head against his shoulders and neck, I was overcome with the first flickers of sexual feelings and secretly planted a kiss on the nape of his neck. I don't think he noticed anything, but for me it might as well have been a formal engagement. From that moment on, until after I turned fourteen, I was true to my "beloved" and fantasized about the time when he would finish medical school and I would be old enough to be his wife. All of a sudden being a girl did not seem quite so bad.

The weeks went by too fast, but I had grown, gained some muscle, gotten a lovely tan, and felt strong and good, inside and out.

On my return to Stuttgart, the Post family was in the middle of moving to Greece. I could not imagine life without Nicoline. She felt as sad as I did. One afternoon, on the side of the empty pool, we cut ourselves above the wrist, mingled our blood, and very seriously promised each other that if we became mothers one day and had daughters, we would name them after each other. My first child was a girl, and in 1962 I had a tiny, brand-new Nicoline in my life. Eventually I lost touch with the original one, but I recently found her again, living in Switzerland, married with two children, a boy and a girl named Rhea. She tells me that she had totally forgotten our solemn promises to each other about the naming of our daughters. So, there was no new Sabina, but in any case my Nicoline loves her name.

CHAPTER 28

Education is not the filling of a pail,
But the lighting of a fire.

—W. B. Yeats (1865–1939)

During the summer, Father found a nice, brand-new apartment in a three-family house in Bad Cannstatt, about twenty minutes by tram from his shop. All this happened while I was at Grandmother's in Eningen. Shortly after my return we moved. I can't say I was thrilled. I had gotten used to our living arrangements at the Neuwirths' house. I had my friend Eva so close by and my beloved Silberpappelweg, the gateway to so many adventures. Moving also meant a new *Gymnasium* and not being able to see *Onkel* Otto and *Tante* Marga as often, who lived only half an hour away on foot.

But Mother was very excited at the prospect of a real bathroom with a tub and hot water and a washing machine in the basement, which was used by three families. We had the first floor, a kitchen, a bathroom, a small bedroom for Mother, a larger room for Tina and me, and a living/dining room with glass doors leading onto a small terrace. In the attic there was a tiny room with a closet, just big enough for a single bed, a chair, and a small table. This was to be Gabi's room, and I envied her the total privacy and independence. There was nothing grand about the apartment, but we were no longer poor refugees dependent on other people.

Tina and I would have liked it better if Father had not been present so much. With him around, the tension in the house was dreadful and cast a dark shadow over our lives. Mother tried hard to play happy family, hoping to create a nice, normal home life for us, but I could see that she was unhappy, feeling the strain of the rather shaky marriage. Father did not know how to relate to us and would go from being a strict authoritarian figure to hardly noticing us at all.

In September Mother took me to the *Mädchen* (girls) *Gymnasium* in Bad Cannstatt to enroll me. The building looked austere with its dark-red sandstone, like dried blood. But it turned out to be a great place of learning for me. Many of our teachers were unemployed university professors. The whole system of higher education had been disrupted by the war, and these professors faced the challenge of teaching a much younger audience than they had encountered before. To them we were practically children.

Sometimes they did not get it quite right, like our physics instructor, who was unable to teach elementary physics, especially to girls. He just filled the entire blackboard with obscure formulas. But most of our teachers were superb and threw themselves wholeheartedly into the task of inspiring and awakening our young minds.

The school had an excellent music program, the director of which, Maestro Rudolph Stein, had conducted a symphony orchestra before the war. He barely survived a bomb attack and had to have a metal plate put into his head. This would give him "funny turns," during which he either collapsed or flipped into another reality for a few moments—which meant that his career in the concert hall was finished. He could, however, teach, and he left a marvelous musical legacy for all of us.

The first time I attended his class, he played the first two movements of Beethoven's *Moonlight Sonata* without telling us the title or the composer. Our task was to describe what we had heard, what we felt while listening to it, and how we would recount the experience to someone who had never heard this kind of music. Then he started to take parts of the sonata and play it in the style of seventy years earlier, the time of Bach, followed by the style of twenty or thirty years later—the romantic era, and then a hundred years later. Thus our ears got accustomed to the different styles of music ranging from the baroque era to twentieth-century composers like Stravinsky and Berg. In no time we learned to identify and appreciate music styles of all periods and, gradually, the individual "handwritings" of the major composers. For me it was the beginning of a lifelong interest and love for music, another dimension I could escape into.

During late morning, Dr. Stein often arranged for us to go to rehearsals of the Stuttgart Symphony Orchestra. I was able to see many distinguished guest conductors, like Wilhelm Furtwängler, Herbert von Karajan, and a very young rookie conductor from Spain, Rafael Frühbeck de Burgos. He was rehearsing Schubert's *Unfinished Symphony* for that evening's performance. The dashing young Spaniard infected the orchestra with his humor and passion, and I remember much laughter back and forth, as well as misunderstandings because of the maestro's funny German pronunciation. It all made such an impression on me that I never forgot his long, rather cumbersome name.

In April of 2006, when staying in Washington, DC, I heard Maestro Frühbeck de Burgos conduct the Washington Symphony at the Kennedy Center. Through our hosts I had the opportunity to meet him backstage after the concert. It was close to fifty years since I had last seen him. He was less dashing, a bit portly, and had lost most of his beautiful dark hair. His face, however, was as radiant as before, and his eyes expressed the same passion and humor I had remembered for so long. When I told him what an impression he had made on a sixteen-year-old girl in Germany, he hugged me warmly and spoke of the concert tour to Stuttgart. Strange how some of the threads of one's life can reconnect so unexpectedly.

Dr. Stein also directed our school chamber orchestra, which consisted of violins, a cello, flutes, oboes, and clarinets. The missing instruments he would quite masterfully represent on the piano, from which he also conducted, the way Mozart had done.

Dr. Stein had great ambitions for us. My strong alto voice, musical ear, and enthusiasm allowed me to join his operatic singers. *Onkel* Hermann had given me a head start.

Our student ensemble performed wonderful operas in the years I

Sabina as Village Barber
in *Der Dorfbarbier*
(standing)

Sabina as Village Barber
(hands above head)

Sabina as Village Barber (middle)

was at the *Gymnasium*. Dr. Stein managed to rent costumes and wigs for us from the Stuttgart state opera. With some safety pins and false hems we somehow made them fit us. I mostly played the male leads, the tenor parts, despite being relatively short.

We performed *Der Dorfbarbier* (*The Village Barber*) by Johann Baptist Schenk, who had been Beethoven's teacher. The opera is a forerunner of the later *Barber of Seville* by Gioachino Rossini. Dr. Stein's wife, who had been an opera singer once, gave me singing lessons at their home and taught me how to move and act onstage while singing and paying attention to the conductor and the orchestra. I don't know which I liked better, the singing or the acting, but in my mind I saw a career on the stage looming ahead. Our performance was a great success and got rave reviews in many newspapers. Father came to the premiere and showed a lot of interest in me all of a sudden. He took me out to a very fancy restaurant, treating me as if I was his young mistress. The way he helped me in and out of my coat, brushing my small breasts with his hands, felt very uncomfortable and confusing. It makes me cringe with disgust even now. He had done the same with Tina a year before. Evidently, it was all he knew; after a life of sleaze, such behavior was second nature to him. Oh, how I despised him!

The teacher who had the greatest influence on us and who became our role model was Professor Vera Kaufmann. She was not a particularly beautiful woman with her dark hair pulled back tightly into a small bun and an angular face, which looked classical in profile with her sharp nose. But when she looked at you through her horn-rimmed glasses and you caught a spark from her lively eyes, you suddenly felt warm and loved and knew that she really saw you and liked who you were.

She taught chemistry and was our homeroom teacher through the many years until we sat for our *Abitur* (the equivalent of a two-year college degree) at age eighteen or nineteen. She was a spinster by choice, I always felt. She dedicated herself not only to teaching us science but even more to helping us to avoid some of the pitfalls of adolescence, to develop our minds, and to learn to be faithful to our own individuality and uniqueness. We loved her!

Unfortunately, she had a clubfoot—her only imperfection and obvious for all to see. The rest of her was so honest and true. In fact, I envied her because my "clubfoot" seemed to be buried deep inside me.

English was the most important subject for me; I had not given up my dream to go to America one day. Our teacher, a caricature of the proverbial spinster, was Miss Plickert, who also taught us French in her dry and humorless fashion. She was obsessed with homework assignments, which she marked up with the precision of a brain surgeon.

Herr Günter, who taught history, taught me very little. He was so gross to look at, with his greasy hair parted in the middle, in an equally greasy dark-brown suit, the fly of which was open more times than not. As if this was not enough, he reeked of stale smoke, and his yellow stained teeth and fingers gave him a sickly and disgusting look. He seldom noticed that I skipped many of his classes, so I never really found out the answers to the "Irish Question" or the "Schleswig Holstein Question," or any other questions. My knowledge about European history stayed pretty rudimentary until I became an adult. We learned little about American history, which would have interested me much more.

There were a few Catholics in my class, and once a week we had a visiting chaplain, Dr. Birk, come and instruct us. He was maybe in his midthirties and painfully shy, so, of course, we mischievous teenage girls exploited his weakness by asking embarrassing questions concerning matters of procreation and the Immaculate Conception. After an hour of torture, the poor man would leave with his face and neck bright red to his ears. But the following week he was back, and he continued to teach year after year, maybe seeing his ordeal as a testing of his faith.

In fact, as we grew older and more mature, we established a good relationship with him. Several times, during school vacation, he arranged wonderful trips by bus, often for several days, to view churches and cathedrals all through Germany, Switzerland, and France, culminating in seeing Le Corbusier's masterpiece in Ronchamp, France. I learned so much about the history of church architecture, monastic life in the Middle Ages, and the sacrifices that were made to build these magnificent edifices. A few years ago I heard that Dr. Birk had died, and I wish I could have thanked him for all he did for us.

I had settled in well at my new school, which served as an oasis while I entered the strange and confusing territories of puberty, like sex and my changing body. Like all teens I was trying to find out who I might be under it all and who I might become, and I was mourning the relatively carefree years of my later childhood, where the present was mostly so much stronger and colorful than the past, and the future too foggy to think much about. All that was changing, and I was afloat in a world I no longer felt familiar in.

CHAPTER 29

... and pluck till time and times are done,
The silver apples of the moon,
The golden apples of the sun.

—W. B. Yeats (1865–1939),
"The Song of Wandering Aengus,"
from *The Wind Among the Reeds* (1899)

At home our lives were gradually improving, as Father's store was producing a small but steady income, and Mother kept an eye on the money whenever she could. Father was pretty lackadaisical about taking money out of the register at the end of the day, feeling it was all profit and there to spend as he saw fit.

One day Mother and Father had a big argument about whether I could have a new pair of shoes for school; I needed shoes that actually fit me properly. Up until that time, I had been the third wearer of shoes handed down by my two sisters after they had outgrown them. Once, when we still lived in Degerloch and I complained that the worn-out shoes pinched my toes, Mother had begged for some money to get me new ones. But Father just picked up the old trotters, took them into the kitchen, and cut the toe section out with a sharp knife, right there on the bread board. I had to go to school with my sock-encased toes sticking out for all to see. I was cruelly teased and humiliated.

Finally, a school friend's mother gave me a pair of black boots with metal toecaps, which had belonged to one of her sons and were barely worn. I wore them for a long time with skirts and dresses. Those boots made me feel very strong, and I threatened to kick anyone who so much as said anything in the shin. That seemed to settle it.

A LONG SILENCE

More and more goods were now available for purchase, as the "German economic miracle" developed with the aid of American funds. Mother bought a gallon of sunflower-yellow paint and transformed all our battleship-gray bedroom furniture: bedsteads, lockers, and table and chairs, all of which were military issue. What a big difference it made. Our joy was marred, however, by the injuries to Mother's hands. She had used a solution of strong caustic soda to strip off the gray gloss paint, not knowing that she needed to protect her hands with rubber gloves. By the time she felt pain, her hands were raw and bleeding. She had to keep them bandaged up for nearly a week, but as soon as they had healed, she started painting again with great abandon.

Then the sewing project began. Curtains, bedcovers with ruffles, lampshades, and a tablecloth, all in bright stripes of red, yellow, white, and soft gray, made the whole room look cheerful and light. Tina and I felt pampered like young princesses and lay on our beds for hours, admiring the splendor. If only Mother had not had to suffer so much to achieve it.

It was nice to share a room with Tina, even though we fought over space sometimes and my untidiness drove her crazy. Tina seemed quite grown-up (she was fifteen) and had a romance going—harmless, of course—with a boy who lived a few houses down the street. She appeared more settled and communicative now, and we often laughed over absolutely nothing until our sides nearly split.

Father had brought home an old gramophone and a pile of 33- and 78-rpm records. We were not allowed to use the machine or listen to the records, especially the one called *Die Dreigroschenoper* (The Threepenny Opera) by Kurt Weill and Bertolt Brecht. This was, of course, like an invitation to listen to it at the first possible opportunity we had. It was very strange music and even stranger singing. The words did not make a lot of sense to me, and they were eerily unsettling and slightly frightening, enough so that I remember some of them to this day:

> Und die minderwertige Witwe,
> (and the underage widow),
> deren Namen niemand weiss,

(whose name no one knows),
wachte auf und war geschändet,
(woke up having been violated),
Mackie welches war dein Preis?
(Mackie, what was your price?)

There were other songs about soldiers, cannons, sharks with large teeth, and the music was always anxiety-provoking and strangely fascinating at the same time.

The other records were mostly classical music, like Beethoven's Violin Concerto, the First Piano Concerto by Tchaikovsky, Smetana's *My Fatherland*, some Wagner, and piano music by various composers. Apart from Wagner, I listened to this music over and over, until I knew every note and pause. Often they made me cry and think of Volkart, my beloved, and the Kinderhaus am Hohenwald.

For Mother, being able to listen to good music became a sort of therapy. Her feelings of loss and deep pain found expression in Chopin's ballades or Schubert's *Winterreise* or some similar stirring piece. I would sometimes steal into the living room, where she was sitting at the ironing board, entranced by a particular passage. Silent tears were slowly gliding down her face, while the hot iron singed a brown diamond shape on a white napkin or a blouse. Only when she smelled the burning cloth did she come back from where the music had transported her and scold herself for being so careless.

She was actually superb at ironing. No wrinkles were tolerated in skirts, shirts, tablecloths, pants, blouses, pajamas, and handkerchiefs, all of which were swiftly smoothed to perfection by her skilled handling of the silver iron. It seems to me now as if she was trying to flatten out the traumas and upheavals of her entire life. With the back-and-forth of the iron and deep concentration, she appeared determined to make the rough terrain of her life orderly and pristine, flat and predictable, so there'd be no dangerous pitfalls left. Unconsciously she was erasing the pain, the shame, and the terror.

Mother ironed with great passion right up to her death in 1992, and since then both my daughter Nicoline and I have taken up ironing in memory of her—she in Europe and I in the United States. It has become a way to be close to Mother and honor her life, while providing me with quiet time to follow my own thoughts, let the first line of a poem settle on me, or flatten out some of the troubling things in the world, if only for a few moments.

CHAPTER 30

**I would like to paint my body red and go out into
The glittering snow to die.**

—Mary Oliver (1935–),
from "Tecumseh," "American Primitive" (1983),
New and Selected Poems (1992)

In 1954, our entire school went to one of the movie theaters in Bad Cannstatt. We were to see a documentary film about recent German history and were told it would show what happened under Adolf Hitler and the Nazis.

I was actually quite excited to see my third film ever. The first had been Walt Disney's *Bambi* some years before, and I recalled how sad it was. The second one was an advertising film for a soap powder called "Persil" and was a funny farce. It featured the then-famous Zarah Leander, who sang romantic songs in her deep, slightly suggestive voice; I was never quite sure whether she was a man or a woman. I had seen the film several times with my friend Nicoline, first because it was free and second because we were fascinated with the realism of moving pictures, which appeared as if everything was happening right in front of your eyes.

I was, however, not prepared for the realism of the documentaries we were about to see. The footage had been smuggled out of Germany to Sweden before the war ended. That is where the Allies took possession of it.

The lights went out, and there I was in the middle of a gruesome scene. Hundreds of people emerged from long rows of barracks and were herded across a muddy yard toward a brick building. A German officer's voice explained things in a rather matter-of-fact way, stressing the German efficiency and ingenuity of the whole process without referring to the terribly emaciated people at all. They were dressed in striped suits that looked like pajamas. As they dragged themselves along, some could barely walk and others were beaten by soldiers with rifle butts.

Next I saw these terrified people undress at gunpoint, and then, totally naked, they were pushed into a large hall, men, women, and children clinging to each other. I remember their frightened hollow eyes and how closely they were packed. They were told that they would be getting a delousing shower. How on earth could they clean themselves in such a crowded space? I wondered.

The next footage showed heaps of naked, contorted corpses being pulled out of the building with large iron hooks; some were put to one side so that a few emaciated but still-living men in striped pajamas could cut off the women's hair and throw it on an already huge heap. I started to feel nauseous. The commentator proudly announced that in the German Reich nothing was wasted and that the hair would be used to stuff pillows and to make soap. Other prisoners came with large wheelbarrows and carts, threw the limp bodies on them, and rolled the corpses across a street to another building with two large chimneys for cremation, "a rather hygienic way to get rid of refuse."

Seeing the lifeless bodies, like rag dolls with their arms, legs, and necks in unnatural positions as they were tipped out and shoveled into the hot burning chambers, was the most gruesome thing to watch. It was so unimaginable and horrific that I spaced out. I fainted and then buried my face in my lap with thumbs blocking my ears.

I don't remember anything else, or how I got home after the screening. I went straight to bed and pulled the sheets over my head, but the images would not go away and never have.

That day was the end of my second childhood, the one that had been so hard to resurrect. From now on nothing would ever be the same. Not only had the film triggered my own personal trauma, but it threw me with great force into a suffocating mixture of tremendous guilt and shame, from which I am only now, by speaking about it, slowly emerging.

All the good things that had happened in the last few years now seemed like a dream. I was back in a place of horror and pain, and fear so heavy and dark enveloped me that I felt I was suffocating. Mother thought I was just sick and kept me in bed for the remainder of the week.

Later, a school friend told me that the Allies had decided that all young Germans must see these documentaries so that nothing so horrific could ever happen again. The program had lasted for just a short time, as many children were quite traumatized by the horrific images. We were not a television generation and therefore not numbed to seeing violence and death on a flickering screen. Anyway, the program had targeted the wrong population. We had been infants, toddlers, and small children when these atrocities had been committed. It would have been better to show these films to those who had been adults during the Holocaust, those who might have known something, or suspected, and done nothing.

Mother eventually found out what I had seen and didn't really believe what I told her. "If they had done this, we would have known. How could something so terrible have been kept secret?" was her response. It took her a long time to accept the unthinkable.

From that time on, I became really uncomfortable being a German, and I looked at adults—especially men—for example, shopkeepers, our postman, tram conductors, and just men in the street, with great suspicion. "Is he one of them who did these terrible things?" was a question in the forefront of my mind.

I started to feel ashamed to belong to a country that had allowed something so abominable to happen. I wanted none of it, and I made a decision to leave Germany as soon as I became an adult at twenty-one. I also experienced deep anger at what I understood of German society. The orderliness and obedience to authority made me feel sick. The signs in the park, like *Rasen betreten ist verboten* (Walking on the lawn is forbidden), infuriated me. I thought maybe there had once been signs that stipulated *Juden retten ist verboten* (Saving Jews is forbidden). But most Germans wouldn't have needed this spelled out; they must have known it anyway, as only a few disobeyed the implicit law.

On top of everything, I felt extremely guilty at having survived those awful times when so many did not. I really had no right to complain or even talk about what happened to us; after all, we were alive. So it was better never to talk about it.

My sister Tina's reaction was the same, maybe even stronger. She experienced extreme survivor's guilt and identification with the Holocaust victims. "I wish I had been killed in a concentration camp," was her response. She was so attuned to people's suffering, so introverted and psychologically unprotected that the Holocaust and subsequent wars or catastrophic conditions in other parts of the world made her extremely despondent and angry, mostly at her own impotence and because she did not know how to help or stop the inhumanities.

My sister Gabi had already left school and was not subjected to the experimental "treatment."

From what I can remember, there was little or no discussion at school about the documentary we had seen. Maybe I had just shut off to any more traumas or to even talking about it. It seemed as though life just went on as before. For me, though, it never quite did. But like many others, I entered the Big Silence, a silence of dirtying, slimy shame and of granite-hard guilt, which encased us like heavy armor.

I am only now beginning to understand why it took me nearly fifty years to start talking about the war and the postwar period.

At home there was a lot of tension and unhappiness. Father had taken up his old lifestyle: womanizing, staying out most nights, and returning to our apartment in the early hours. He slept on the couch in the living room, which we made up for him every evening, and Mother always left him a plate of small snacks and a glass of milk, next to an ironed white napkin on the coffee table. She was so disgusted with him that she slept alone on a single bed in the small room. In the morning when we got up, we had to creep around so as not to wake the ogre. Before I left for school, my job was to clean, wax, and polish his shoes, which he left for me on the small kitchen balcony. God help me if I did not do them perfectly.

Sometimes he did not come home at all, which made Mother cry. Once he was gone for many days. Going through his passport later, she discovered that he had flown to Caracas, Venezuela, to be with a former mistress—a doctor—who had recently moved there.

He began to live a more and more lavish life to impress his ever-changing conquests, and his debts grew proportionally. The manufacturers of the merchandise that was sold at his two stores (he had added another one in a different town) were after him, but he made promises and always paid them just enough so they would keep the supply lines going.

Mother basically ran the shop in Bad Cannstatt; the other one was managed by one of his paramours. Father only showed up in the late afternoon, took most of the cash out of the register, drove to the second store in his brand-new Opel, did the same there, and then went out on the town or visited his many adoring women. He was a heavy smoker, and I would imagine that he drank as well. What else do people do when they sit in nightclubs and bars all night?

He developed a crush on the exotic dancer Josephine Baker and followed her all the way to Paris, showering her with roses and orchids, all the time keeping Mother's housekeeping money to the bare minimum and not allowing any unnecessary expenses.

We felt such terrible shame because of him, and as the years went by, everybody seemed to know that Herr de Werth was a Casanova. I sometimes saw him after school in the center of Bad Cannstatt having a late lunch with some woman, or walking in the park like a peacock, immaculately dressed with yet another conquest. It was most humiliating.

Often I wished that he would never come home and that Mother could find a new husband who would love and cherish her. The trouble was that Father, every now and then, felt he had to play the role of paternal figure and disciplinarian. Once during Sunday dinner, when we had the only meat of the week, I got a piece of fatty gristle on my plate, which I cut off and pushed to the side. Father tried to make me eat it. I tried and gagged—I just could not swallow it—so in anger he hit my left hand with his heavy knife so hard that I bled. I was then sent out of the room and had to go hungry.

Another time Tina displeased him about something. He went to get the *Rohrstock* (a thin cane) from the top of Mother's wardrobe, made her lift up her skirt, pull down her panties, and bend over. She was wearing a sanitary belt and pad between her legs for her period; nonetheless, he whipped her, a sixteen-year-old girl, until she had red welts all over her skinny buttocks. That was how I found out that adolescent girls and women have periods once every four weeks.

Not long after this humiliating experience, Tina and I came home together in the early afternoon. We heard the monster splashing in the bathtub; he must have just gotten up and was getting ready for a few hours of collecting money and carousing.

Tina came from the kitchen along the narrow hallway, I from the other end. We stopped in front of the bathroom, saw that the door was unlocked and looked at each other. We both had the same thought for a moment, knowing we could rid ourselves of him forever and release our mother from her sick emotional attachment to him. It would have been easy, we thought, with the element of surprise to rush in and with our combined strength and determination hold him under water. It was a tense moment, neither one of us breathed; then Tina put her hand on my shoulder and looked at me intensely, shaking her head from side to side. It was a moment that left us shocked and drained; we could not speak to each other the rest of the day. In fact we did not speak of this moment until many years later, on a hill in County Connemara, Ireland. And after that, never again.

CHAPTER 31

Tell me, what is it you plan to do
With your one wild and precious life?
—Mary Oliver (1935–),
from "The Summer Day," *New and Selected Poems* (1992)

It was good that we had not murdered our father, and it turned out to be unnecessary as well. For unexpectedly, another man came into Mother's life.

She met him through a new friend—a very interesting woman who was a Unitarian, a writer, and a poet. Her name was Elke Lazarraga, a freckled redhead with horn-rimmed glasses, behind which a pair of blue eyes were in constant motion. She had grown up in Malaga, Spain, the daughter of a Spanish architect and a German mother. Elke's German was delivered with the speed of light and often sounded quite foreign. She was amazingly energetic and enterprising, as well as independent. She was divorced and led a very free life, having a series of passionate romances with other writers and intellectuals.

Just before Carnival week in 1954 she urged Mother to join her at a costume dance the following Monday, where there would be many academics and other interesting people. Mother was reluctant, but Tina and I begged her to go and have some fun. So she sewed herself a skirt out of a jungle-print cotton fabric, which she wore over her black swimsuit. On the afternoon of the dance we covered her legs, arms, back, neck, and face with dark stage makeup to make her look like a South Seas beauty. With red lipstick and her wavy hair down, which she normally wore pinned on the nape of her neck, she looked amazing. A

Mother in Father's shop

Mother in our new home

white flower behind one ear provided the final and perfect touch. When *Tante* Elke came to pick her up in her VW Bug, we practically had to push her out of the front door.

The next day Mother told us that she had danced the whole evening with a very distinguished-looking, tall, and incredibly handsome gentleman. He had been very shy at first but confessed that he was quite taken by her Gauguinesque beauty. Mother explained that the lighting at the dance hall was dimmed and this wonderful and ah, so good-smelling man, John Weitzenberg, took her to be no more than twenty-five years old. She was in fact forty-three. He expressed amazement when he found out that she had three daughters at home, first imagining that they must be infants or toddlers. In any case, I had not seen my mother so young and sparkling since the day, years before, when I glimpsed her dancing with the checkered tablecloth.

A couple of weeks later she met this John for coffee somewhere in town, and afterward they walked in the park. John's wife, Dagmar, had died of a sudden heart attack a couple of years after they had arrived from Reval, Estonia, via Sweden, around 1947. Mother was convinced he was still in love with his Dagmar, with whom he had had a very good marriage. He now lived with his aging mother and his son, Gunnar, a difficult and depressed young man, who was an alcoholic.

Mother then told him about her life and the terrible marriage she was in and about Tina and me. Gabi was spending most of her time, when she was not at work, at the wealthy family home of her boyfriend, Peter, her future husband-to-be, and did not show much interest in us. She was looking for security and respectability, as well as a way out of the situation at home. And who could blame her?

On a late autumn afternoon, when Mother was sitting at the ironing board, she confessed to me how fond she had become of John Weitzenberg. The way she described him made her forget the hot iron, and soon yet another blouse had the telltale light-brown diamond branded on it. This time Mother laughed and was sure that over time the singed spot would fade away. I had never seen her so relaxed. Then she asked me whether I would like to come on an excursion the following Sunday, so

Gabi, John, Mother, Tina, Sabina

I could meet HIM. Mother was not surprised at my instant excitement. I already liked this John, sight unseen, because she was so much happier than before, and some of her old beauty had come back. She was sewing new clothes for herself and wearing lipstick again, and even hats.

So that Sunday we went off to the railway station, Mother, Tina, and I. I spotted him first on the platform waving at us. He was just the way she had described him. But nonetheless I was struck speechless when we shook hands; I just curtsied, awed by his aristocratic looks and stature, his height, over six feet, the silver hair, and such a kind smile that you felt he was genuinely delighted at meeting you. I felt instinctively that there was nothing fake about him and that he could be trusted.

I sat next to him in our train compartment, and before the train had rolled to the first stop on our way to the mountains, he had put me totally at ease. He talked to me with respect and asked questions about my interests and life at school. The best part was he really wanted me to answer him and listened to me with great attention. Mother and Tina sat opposite us, and he even got my shy sister to talk and smile. Mother was beaming.

One of the greatest delights for me was that he spoke fluent English and French, apart from more than a dozen other languages, like Russian, Polish, Finnish, Italian, and Greek. We had a simple conversation in English; he helped me out when I got stuck and we laughed when I used a wrong word. By now I was totally mesmerized by this man with the deep and gentle voice and beautiful hands, who smelled so pleasant. Father's short fingers were always stained yellow from smoking, as were his teeth, and he mostly reeked of smoke and alcohol.

By the time the train brought us to our destination, and we commenced our hike up the mountain to see the *Mädchen Fels* (maiden rock) and the medieval castle above, I was completely enchanted by Mother's new friend. It had started to rain, and we unrolled our plastic ponchos and marched on. John told us the legend of the young girl who had been kidnapped by one of the knights of the castle. Rather than become his wife, the young maiden threw herself off the cliff and fell to her death. The rock had been called the *Mädchen Fels* ever since. Normally a story like that would have made me sad, but I was having such a wonderful time with Mother's new friend and with Tina, who was more cheerful than usual, that nothing, not even the rain, could diminish my joy.

The birches glowed with their wet golden leaves, the sycamores burned like fire, and the ferns under our feet lay bent over in hues of ochre and cinnamon. It smelled of fungi all around us, as we sat on a fallen tree trunk, eating our sandwiches. We sang German songs and laughed a lot. I suddenly had the feeling that we were a real family, just

John Weitzenberg,
"Batjuschka" (Grandfather)

John, in earlier years

Mother, in later years

exactly the way it should be. Meeting Mother's eyes, I saw they were filled with happy tears to the brim, and she nodded at me. I knew she, too, felt that we all belonged with each other.

On the way home, I fell asleep against John's arm and shoulder; only when the locomotive braked did I become aware of where I was and snuggled even closer to him.

After the three of us got home and had taken off our wet clothes, I stood there in my cotton underwear, with hands on my nonexistent hips, and turned to Mother: "*Mutti*, if you don't want him, I shall take him." We laughed at this moment for many years to come.

Three years later, after John had put his old mother into a home, and his thirty-two-year-old son finally moved out, my mother, much to our delight, did take him. John had put money down for a modest apartment, which was still under construction, while Mother divorced my father on grounds of adultery and married John in a civil ceremony.

Mother, Tina, and I could finally leave. Gabi—Father's loyal daughter, a good Catholic, and vehemently opposed to divorce—stayed with him for some years. When her Peter finished medical school, she married him and joined his wealthy family. The relationship between us was never very close.

Father was furious about the divorce and the fact that Mother was remarrying. Who was going to leave him his little snacks when he came home early in the morning? I believe he quite liked the arrangement. Being married meant that the women in his life could have no illusions about a permanent relationship. On top of it, Mother had run his shops almost single-handedly. She was a great asset, and the customers liked to be served by her. She was also cheap; Father never paid her a penny outside the housekeeping money, while he squandered a small fortune.

After the move, Mother left the Catholic Church, where she had been a member only in name, not by conviction. She no longer wanted to pay the church taxes. This created quite a furor. A priest was dispatched in haste to our new apartment with "glad tidings": the pope had excommunicated Mother for divorcing Father, and her marriage to John was invalid. Furthermore, she was living in sin and would be condemned to go to hell for eternity.

My mother, Klarissa, rose to the occasion. She stood up, took a deep breath, and laughed from deep down in her belly. She told this man of God that her God did not condemn women for leaving abusive husbands and situations that hurt her soul and the souls of her daughters. She said a lot of other things about decency, truth, and love. She must have made her dead father, the *Freidenker* (freethinker), very proud. The priest left without uttering another word, like a dog with his tail between his legs. I was so amazed at Mother's courage that I could not speak.

CHAPTER 32

Music is the shorthand of emotion.
—Leo Tolstoy (1828–1910)

The years before we were able to move away from Father were made more palatable because of all the activities connected to life at school. I had slowly moved away from trying to live a religious and church-approved existence. The nearest Catholic Church was a long walk from our apartment. We girls did not go every Sunday, and going to confession became a rare occasion. I had bouts of remorse and guilt about it, but usually I just put those feelings into a remote corner of my awareness. On the surface I was a good schoolgirl planning adventures with my small group of friends.

We were all tomboys and spent time on the slopes of vineyards or in vacant lots along the railway lines, where we smoked our first cigars and cigarettes with much coughing and nausea. The cigars I pilfered from Father's cupboard, and if there were none available, we rolled something to smoke out of all kinds of dried leaves and twigs. Smoking made us feel very tough and invulnerable and afforded us a temporary delay before we had to give in and become young women. Unfortunately, smoking also turned into a habit for me that lasted the next twenty years.

While to most people I appeared agreeable, likable, and often funny, I kept that other part of myself well hidden. It was only when I was alone or at night that I allowed myself to drop down to my other self, where all the guilt and shame took over. I had accumulated so much over the years. There was the guilt of being a failed Catholic, the collective guilt by "virtue" of being German, and the irrational guilt of not having prevented all the horror. The fact that I had been too young and thus impotent to change history gave me no dispensation.

Guilt and shame make good bedfellows; they feed on each other. Germany's atrocities became the "gold standard" against which all other war crimes would be measured.

In the spring of 1955, when I was thirteen and a half, I got my first taste of America, without actually having to cross the Atlantic Ocean. Two girls from our school were chosen to attend an American high school at the nearby US military base for two weeks. I was one of the girls, and I could hardly believe my luck. The base was spread over a large area of Bad Cannstatt. The residential part, which included schools, sports facilities, a cinema, cafeteria, and a large PX store, was the one I had passed on my way to school. So, on our first day, we two German girls went to the gatehouse where the military police guard waved us in, and we were greeted by two American mothers with a daughter each, who were to be our hosts for the duration of our visits.

I had seen several American movies, mostly westerns, and one with Doris Day and Rock Hudson, but they had not prepared me for the foreign world I was entering. Mrs. Porter and her daughter Marilyn had dark smooth skin and were all smiles and appeared to be pleased to welcome me. They were hard to understand at first with their Southern accents.

We walked over to the school, a low building with many windows. Marilyn took me to her classroom. I could hardly believe my eyes. Young pretty girls and young handsome boys sat at individual desks. They all looked fairly casual, lounging around; some had their feet on the desk or another chair, chewing gum, talking, laughing, and just having the best time. I noticed that some of the girls wore rolled up jeans, white bobby socks, and loafers or tennis shoes. The boys wore colorful shirts with their jeans and their hair was cropped so short that it resembled fur. And to my utter astonishment, some of the girls wore earrings and a bit of lipstick. They all welcomed me with a lot of friendly chatter, which I found hard to understand and even harder to respond to.

The door opened and the teacher, a young man in jeans and a short-sleeved shirt, walked in. I jumped to attention, the way we did at school. Nobody else moved, and I sat down in embarrassment. The teacher came over to say hello and ask me whether I was familiar with Shakespeare, because they were reading *Macbeth* at the moment. I told him that we had recently read *Julius Caesar* in class, and he seemed pleased.

It took me awhile to adjust to the laissez-faire attitude of everyone, the relaxed poses, the gum chewing (in my school, we would have had detention for that), but I got over the initial shock and started to follow the lesson. Some words were really hard for me, and I did not have a dictionary to look things up. Everyone had to read a few lines aloud, and I did all right.

At recess, a handsome, freckled boy bought me a long-necked bottle of Coca-Cola. I instantly took to the strange and wonderful taste. I was used to drinking a small bottle of milk at school. For the rest of the morning I felt very perky and animated; the caffeine was doing its job. I learned about President Abraham Lincoln, whose portrait showed a somewhat melancholy but striking-looking man who commanded respect. I had never heard of slavery, and my image of Americans, who could do no wrong in my eyes, was slightly sullied. I looked at Marilyn, the only black student, and I felt bad about what her family must have endured. But at least things were better now.

Marilyn took her assignment as my host very seriously, explaining everything and introducing me to other teachers. She was my own age, but much taller and with large dark-brown eyes. She wore a wide gathered black-and-white polka-dot skirt, white socks, and a sky-blue blouse with white heart buttons. Her skin was the color of café au lait, and her face was framed with black curly hair. I found her very exotic and beautiful.

She took me to her house for lunch. I could not believe how well the Porters lived. The duplex house had two floors with large rooms. Marilyn, an only child, had her own bedroom with a private bathroom upstairs, all in white and pink, frilly curtains, many books and games, and her own radio and record player. I was immediately introduced to the latest rock 'n' roll hits. What a world these Americans had created for themselves, thousands of miles away from home, here in the middle of Germany! It all seemed so lighthearted and pleasant.

Marilyn's mother called us downstairs for lunch. She had made large sandwiches with so much ham and cheese piled in between the bread that it was hard to bite into. There was enough for our whole family in one of those sandwiches, and we had pickles too. I washed it all down with another bottle of Coca-Cola. I could have had tomato juice (they pronounced it "tow-may-tow") but I was already hooked on the sweet, syrupy stuff that made me buzz like a bee inside my head. Before I went home in the afternoon I had yet another dose of the seductive beverage. Later that night, in my bed at home, tossing and turning and unable to sleep or slow down my loudly beating heart and racing mind, I learned about the power of caffeine and decided to keep my consumption to one bottle a day for the next two weeks.

The following day I felt much more at ease at the American school. I liked the unregimented way things were done. The students expressed themselves so easily and freely, asked questions, and had strong opinions. Here I would get a B for conduct and be commended for my enthusiasm. I felt envy, and the idea of me living in such a world and becoming as free as these young people seemed extremely attractive.

Mr. Porter, a noncommissioned officer, took us for lunch at the self-service restaurant, a cafeteria where we could choose from all the different foods displayed. The place was swarming with uniformed men and a few women, so I felt a bit intimidated at first. Marilyn steered me to a counter where large round meat patties sizzled on a grill. She urged me to try her favorite, called a "Davy Crockett," which turned out to be a giant piece of food architecture consisting of a round squishy bun with two thick beef patties separated by melted cheese, tomato slices, onion rings, and lettuce. As if this were not enough, there was bright-yellow mustard and a red sauce called ketchup. I had it all.

Back at our table I picked up this soft, warm tower of food in both hands, salivating, but unable to find a way to put the structure into my mouth. It would have fit into the jaws of a lion. Mr. Porter, who had been watching me with some amusement, took pity on me. "Press down with both hands and bite into the flat part at the edge," he suggested. I must have pressed too hard in my eagerness, because all of a sudden I was sprayed with mustard, ketchup, and meat juice. It ran down my arms to my elbows and dripped onto my skirt, where a slice of tomato had already settled. Marilyn tried to help me with paper napkins (another American triumph), but by now I had thrown caution and good table manners to the wind and dove into the bun with my entire face.

To this day I remember the explosion of tastes in my mouth. It was intoxicating. I hardly paused to take a breath in between bites. When I finally emerged, I had to go to the bathroom and repair the damage as best as I could. Some of my hair had mustard and red speckles. I don't remember much of the afternoon classes; I felt very sleepy, as my body was busy digesting.

Over the next two weeks I had several more "Davy Crockets," lots of ice cream floats, Coca-Cola, and gum. I hardly dared to share my culinary experiences with my family and friends, and I felt a bit guilty about my decadent life behind the fence and guardhouse of Little America. It seems strange to me now that I remember mostly the food, the pastel-colored cars with chrome fins, and the relaxed clothes, instead of the classes I attended. The sensuousness of the whole experience was quite overwhelming and left little room for learning.

One experience, however, taught me something very special. The Porters had invited me to stay with them overnight on the weekend. They were from Alabama, and during my stay I heard a lot about the South and the United States. Mr. Porter's hobby was jazz, and he had a huge record collection. When I showed interest but admitted my ignorance, he gave me a crash course on the history of jazz, illustrated by many musical examples. He ran me through the birth of Negro spirituals and the blues, ragtime and Dixieland, swing and big band, bebop and what was then avant-garde, by artists like Miles Davis, Sonny Rollins, Art Blakey, Dave Brubeck, and the cool music of the Modern

Jazz Quartet. I was thrilled and moved. It was the beginning of my love for jazz, and I shall be forever grateful to my American host for introducing me to it.

When I told Mother about my musical experience at the Porters, I mentioned that they were black Americans. Father, who was home for once, interrupted and said that this was terrible; no daughter of his was allowed to go back to the base and be with "those people." This was the first time I came face-to-face with a racist attitude. Mother expressed her disgust at Father: "These are our liberators! I do not care what color of the rainbow they are; they are fine and decent people." And with that, the matter was closed and I went back for another week.

My English improved a lot, at least in casual conversation. I was now wearing a poodle skirt, which Mother had whipped up overnight on her old Singer machine, along with white socks and tennis shoes. I wore my hair in a ponytail and felt nearly as pretty as my new American schoolmates.

These two weeks made my dream of one day going to America much more real. The base was a little part of America, as were the big cars, the food, the baseball games, and just about everything. The American military wanted its armies to feel at home as much as possible during their long tours abroad. Since that time, they have developed ever-more sophisticated logistical expertise—at astronomical costs, of course—to make war and occupation more tolerable for their troops. South Korea, Vietnam, and now the Emerald City and the Green Zone in Baghdad are impressive examples.

Reentry into the German school system seemed odd. For a few days I was a star in my new outfit and hairstyle. But after a short while, I adapted again to the seriousness, the confinement, and the rigid structure. It was back to bottles of milk, or if we were lucky, milk with cocoa powder. I kept in touch with the Porters for the next year, but then they were transferred to the Philippines, and I lost touch.

CHAPTER 33

Comfort ye, comfort ye my people, says your God.
Speak ye comfortably to Jerusalem
And cry unto her,
That her warfare is accomplished.

—Isaiah 40:1

My overall health and physical development were still not up to the standards of the health department, who pronounced me suffering from "general weakness." Several of my classmates had the same diagnosis, so in August of 1956 we were shipped off to a children's home, St. Norbert, in Rot an der Rot, about fifty kilometers north of Lake Constance. It was a Catholic establishment, run by nuns.

The home was part of a large complex of baroque buildings and was attached to a vast church with two onion-domed spires. On the other side of the church was a monastery where an order of Dutch Cistercian monks lived. I was very intrigued by them; they looked so otherworldly and pure in their white robes. We usually saw them only at Mass, which we attended daily. On our side it was mostly lessons in the morning and afternoon walks through woods and meadows for our health. The nuns ran a tight ship; going to the bathroom meant having to ask for two pieces of toilet paper, which I found embarrassing and not sufficient.

We girls speculated endlessly about why the nuns lived so close to the monks. It seemed rather puzzling and unorthodox, as well as a bit too convenient. We were all in the full blossom (more like a tornado, really) of puberty, and sexual topics were much in our confused minds.

St. Norbert's children's home was not like my little piece of paradise in the Austrian Alps, and I knew Uncle Marshall had had nothing to do with it. Food was plentiful but quite bad, consisting of bread and red jam, thin peppermint tea, and a slightly sour, fatty hash with potatoes and cabbage for the midday meal. Sometimes we had a thick gray soup, which tasted of nothing. I realized how well off I must be that I could criticize the food, as did the other girls. Gone were the days of constant hunger, as I had entered a phase in my life where the availability of food was not constantly in my thoughts.

The four weeks at St. Norbert's revived my interest in religion, at least temporarily. I had not been a good Catholic, but here I could go to Mass every day and receive Holy Communion, as well as go to confession whenever I felt like it. The nuns loved to see me act so piously. For me it meant some quiet time from the nuns and the more than forty girls. I loved to sit in the vast space and let my eyes wander up to the vaulted, beautifully painted ceilings; or marvel at the intricately carved choir benches near the altar; or follow the pattern and colors created by the stained glass windows, with the help of the afternoon sun, on the normally dull flagstones. The smell of incense and candle wax was always in the air, and sometimes a monk would play softly on the old organ.

During one Sunday sermon I developed a little crush on a particular monk. He wore his hair in the style I had seen on one of Napoleon Bonaparte's portraits. He often sat in one of the confessionals, and I made my way to him. I loved his raspy Dutch accent and learned to engage him in conversation by asking for answers to my many doubts. My main motive was to get his attention, I believe. He tried to steer me away from my "dangerous" and "unanswerable" questions by giving me extra Our Fathers and Hail Marys, but a few days later I would be back with more pesky questions, just to be near my "Napoleon." For me it was exciting, even daring, and something to look forward to. I was so hungry for fatherly attention and acknowledgment; my behavior had little to do with piety. Had they known my motives, the nuns would probably have judged it sinful.

It is strange how certain small events are forever etched in one's

SABINA DE WERTH NEU

Cloister in Rot an der Rot

mind. One day, on a walk through the village of Rot, a few of us girls came across a procession of mourners dressed in black, walking behind a black cart on which stood a draped coffin, pulled by a dapple-gray horse. Everyone was mumbling the rosary. It sounded like a hive of bees. The sky was of the clearest, deepest blue, and the trees along the road had already started to display yellow and crimson leaves. The black of the funeral procession was in such a sharp contrast under the late August sun that I felt my heart ache. I experienced a moment of grief over the loss of someone unknown to me and imagined my own death, my body lying in a draped coffin in total darkness, despite the splendor of light and color outside. "When death comes to me one day, I want it to be just like this," I thought to myself. That image has stayed with me to this day.

I shared a crammed dormitory with seven other girls. We were allowed to use the bathrooms only at certain times. During the night we had to use the chamber pots under our beds. We could brush our teeth and wash our hands and faces in the morning and at night. Each Saturday we were given a lukewarm bath, in our underwear, with two nuns present. The big chunk of soap didn't make suds and produced a gray, fatty film on the surface of the water. Getting out was quite a performance. One nun held a towel for the front, the other for the back, as we wriggled out of our wet and clinging underwear. At no point were we permitted to look at our pubescent bodies, as that would only lead to sin. When dry, we were issued clean underwear from the supply of four sets we had brought with us. This bath had to last us for the entire week. Here at St. Norbert's, cleanliness was certainly not next to godliness.

I became more critical about the way the Church interpreted the New Testament. I could not believe that God wanted us to be ashamed of our bodies, which, according to the Bible, he had created in his own image. I often kneeled in the pews of the church, asking Jesus on the cross to answer my questions. I asked in such a way that it just required a yes or no to respond. Jesus could set the record straight by nodding or shaking his head from side to side, ever so slightly. I stared at the face on the cross, not even blinking so as not to miss his answer. All I got from it was swollen red eyes. Part of me knew that it was a sin to test the Son of God in such a way. It just added more to my repertoire of failures.

On one of our last nights, just before 3:00 a.m., we filed into the church to hear the monks sing Gregorian chants, which they did several times during the night. The whole nave vibrated with their rising voices, which seemed to come out of one unearthly body. The old strange chants gave me shivers of joy I had never experienced before. I was overcome with the longing to be a monk, to wear the cream-colored hooded robe and a rope as a belt, just like these mysterious monks. How peaceful it would be to merge with their voices and become one.

CHAPTER 34

**This blessed plot, this earth, this realm,
this England . . .**

—William Shakespeare (1564–1616),
from *Richard II*, act 2, scene 1, I.50 (1595)

In August, before my sixteenth birthday, my English pen pal, Maureen Lawrence, invited me to visit her in Broadstairs, Kent, UK, for two weeks.

All year I had worked hard after school to earn the money for the train fare. *Onkel* Hermann had taught me how to be an entrepreneur and find opportunities to earn some money. I had started to tutor students from the lower grades in English and French, often two or three together, at reduced hourly rates, but it more than doubled my income. The school allowed me to use an empty classroom after school.

Another source of cash flow came from recycling all the boxes and other packing materials from the back of Father's shop. This meant collapsing the boxes and packing them tightly into our old wooden cart, securing it with rope, and pulling it for about two miles to a recycling place near the railway lines. It was weighed, and I often came away with close to fifteen deutsch marks.

I can't say I enjoyed this, since it was hard work and I was very afraid that someone I knew might see and make fun of me. But I did it once a month and put the money into the savings box under my bed. It felt good to have my own money, to buy an occasional ice cream, and to indulge my obsession with movies, mostly American westerns (synchronized by German actors, as subtitles were not popular then).

A LONG SILENCE

Maureen and her parents met me off the ferry in Dover. I felt high from the channel crossing, my first experience with the ocean. On the crossing I felt as if I were leaving everything I knew behind. I suddenly was less burdened by German history and my German identity, as I was listening to the many different languages of the passengers: Dutch, French, and English.

Mr. Lawrence took my suitcase when I emerged through customs. The family took me across the street to a fish-and-chip place on the harbor front. The shrieking of the seagulls was deafening, as they swooped among the crowds. The first thing I had when we sat down was "a nice cup of tea, for you dear," as Mrs. Lawrence told me. The tea was dark, strong, and bitter, but with enough sugar and a dash of milk it momentarily tasted delicious.

I then had two fillets of Dover sole, deep-fried and very fresh and moist, as well as a mountain of finger-thick fried potato sticks, called chips. Maureen suggested I sprinkle salt and vinegar on them. With my usual gusto, I ate everything on my plate. The Lawrences asked me a lot of questions, some of which I just did not understand. Anyway, I could not answer much, as I was too busy eating and could not speak with my mouth full.

After our refreshment we took the train to Broadstairs. The English trains were very cozy; each car had separate compartments, which one entered from the platform. The seats were covered in patterned velour and extremely comfortable. Outside the window the countryside looked very different from what I was used to; I saw the greenest rolling hills, with sheep in large fields enclosed by natural drystone walls. There were small, compact villages, where most of the houses were built of red brick and sat close together, each surrounded by the most lovingly tended gardens.

Maureen was much amused by my English pronunciation. She was a typical English rose and much prettier than she appeared in the photo she had sent me. Her very light skin was slightly freckled; her cheeks had a faint blush that accentuated her nearly transparent blue eyes; and her reddish-blonde, curly hair was almost out of control. We got on well with each other instantly.

Her father was a civil servant and went off to London every morning on an early train in his dark suit, bowler hat, umbrella, and black briefcase. But before he left the semidetached house, he woke each of us up by knocking on our bedroom doors and coming in with "early morning tea and a lovely biscuit, dear." He left a floral china cup and saucer with a chocolate-covered cookie on the bedside table. The first morning I was speechless and very drowsy; after all, there was just the faintest glimmer of daylight coming through the curtains. But I soon got used to this wonderful service, especially the chocolate-covered digestive biscuit.

Mrs. Lawrence was very gracious and had planned a whole itinerary for my visit. We went to the beach close by, and I swam in saltwater for the first time. England was suffering under a rare heat wave, and so the sea breezes were wonderful. We went to London many times, where I saw everything a tourist must see, including London from the top of the Monument after climbing endless stairs. I liked the red double-decker buses; the jolly policemen with their pointed helmets; and Lyon's teahouses, where we refreshed ourselves frequently with more tea and biscuits.

Maureen and I really liked each other. I remember how much we laughed, often about nothing in particular, and how just looking at each other could set us off. Our laughter expressed all the feelings we were unable to put into words at our tender age; it just bubbled out of us like a fountain. I went on my first camping trip with Maureen's Girl Guide (Girl Scout) troop somewhere in the English countryside for three nights. We cooked and even dug a latrine, with canvas curtains around it. It was primitive, but well organized, down to the last detail. We sang a lot and sweltered in our sleeping bags in the damp summer heat. I never forgot the attack of hundreds of earwigs one night that came into our tent during a thunderstorm. We got hysterical and ran outside, trying to brush them off. There was no sleep after that.

Mrs. Lawrence taught me how to make a lemon meringue pie (out of a packet) and how to make chips (French fries). Now I could astonish my mother when I got home, which I did.

A LONG SILENCE

Looking back, the thing I liked most about Britain was that it was so utterly different from Germany. It wasn't just that the mailboxes were painted fire-engine red, or that people lined up in orderly queues, or all the other things that intrigue the first-time visitor to the British Isles. For me the difference was that I did not feel the same intensity and desperation behind everything, none of the struggle and seriousness that invaded every sphere of my life at home.

It wasn't that the English were particularly laissez-faire or relaxed, but they showed a cheery acceptance of the way things were, whether it was bad weather or having to rebuild what the Nazis had bombed. Maybe the fact that they had not lost a war and knowing they had overcome great difficulties and fought with everything they had to save their beloved country (with the help of their friends, the Americans) gave them a healthy and proud optimism. You could practically touch it; I had never experienced so much positive feeling and jolliness in Germany.

On this emerald island I was able to forget, for two long weeks, my shame of having been born a German, my guilt of belonging to a people who had committed such atrocities in the 1930s and 1940s.

In later years, when I hitchhiked through much of Europe, I learned to hide my nationality. It was my experience that anyone who didn't do so would immediately be labeled and even shunned. Being German was synonymous with the Holocaust and being responsible for two world wars. So I denied my origins by posing as Swiss, Finnish, Icelandic, or Norwegian, all countries that had no baggage attached to them. Several times I was exposed as a liar and impostor (and God knows what else) by the arrival of someone who could speak the language of the country I was pretending to be from. One rainy day in rural Wales I was thrown out of a car when the driver discovered that I was German.

Even recently, when I went to the hospital for a small procedure and met the surgeon (who I thought could have been Jewish), I shocked myself by continuing to lie. When asked where my charming accent came from, I answered without hesitating: "From Switzerland," as I have for nearly fifty years. As soon as I said it, I wanted to take it back, but how could I?

I never developed a sense of national identity, and pride was out of the question for many of us. After the war, our national holiday became July 20, in remembrance of the failed assassination of Hitler, hardly a day to make one feel proud and happy.

I started to look at the occupation of West Germany by the Allies as no longer simply acts of tremendous generosity, but also as a strong statement that we could not be trusted, and rightfully so.

I came to loathe German efficiency and the country's ability to run such a well-oiled bureaucracy. So what if they could build beautifully engineered cars? That same efficiency and reliability also enabled the Nazis to systematically eradicate most of Europe's Jewry.

As I had been so heartily welcomed by Maureen and her parents, I, in turn, invited Maureen to come and stay with me in Bad Cannstatt the following summer. I was hoping that by then Mother would have her divorce, and Tina and I would be living with the marvelous John Weitzenberg, whose English was impeccable.

John spoke so many languages; by the time he died in 1979, at age seventy-eight, we counted sixteen, and he was just getting proficient in Chinese Mandarin, Korean, and Japanese, just for the fun of it. John was a geophysicist and had been a captain in the Estonian navy. He grew up in Estonia and St. Petersburg, Russia, where his father was a diplomat to the last tsar, Nicholas. His mother, a Baltic German, spoke German with him and his father, Russian. He had a Polish nanny, a French governess, and an English tutor. The summers were spent at their vacation home in Finland, where he learned to speak Finnish. By the time he entered the Academy at age eleven, he already spoke six languages. His study of Latin laid the foundation for the Romance languages and classical Greek allowed him to pick up modern Greek later on. As Finnish and Hungarian are related, he studied Hungarian too, and so it went.

If that were not enough, he had a passion for world history; in this area, his knowledge was phenomenal. So it was no wonder that I wanted to show him off. He cured Mother of her hatred for the Russian language by reciting love poems by Lermontov and whole passages from

Chekhov, all by heart, in his deep resonant voice. Mother could not believe that what she was hearing was Russian. It sounded so different from the shouting and brutal sounds that had come out of our captors' mouths. So she ended up falling in love with Russian, which sounded like music and tenderness from John's lips, and which healed some of her wounds, I am sure.

John allowed us to call him *Batjuschka* (Grandfather), as he was ten years older than Mother, and he called me *Galubuschka* (little dove). My heart always jumped for joy when he called me that.

After the war, *Batjuschka* had tried to get a job as an interpreter or translator in the diplomatic service of the new Federal Republic of Germany in Bonn. He took it very badly when they did not hire him, and he never found out on what grounds he was rejected. He had fought the Bolsheviks on the side of the White Russians when he was still at school. The family then went to live on their estates in Estonia, and John entered the Estonian navy fighting the Soviets during World War II. He concluded that the people in Bonn might have taken him for a Russian spy. So he never worked again on a regular basis. Translating foreign books into German did not pay much. He lived on a modest pension, supplemented by some money his family had kept with some relatives in Sweden.

In April of 1958 the divorce from Father became final, and Mother married her John in a civil ceremony. From sheer happiness she looked ten years younger than her forty-seven years. Unfortunately, we could not move out until the new apartment was ready. Those last few months were very tense and awkward. Father got really mean, and Tina and I stayed out of his way as much as possible. I often stayed overnight with my school friend Ines, who was an only child and lived with her widowed mother.

In late July we finally moved into our new home. It was on the other side of Bad Cannstatt, not a particularly nice neighborhood, but on one side vineyards and orchards with public footpaths invited us outside to enjoy the air and views. I now had a very long walk to school, about forty-five minutes; during bad weather in the winter I could take two different trams to get closer to school, but I still had a long walk, so it did not save me any time.

I had met a very nice boy from the boys' *Gymnasium* on my old way to school, and we had become close friends, but now we could not see each other that often. His name was Frieder, and he was a year older than me, tall and quite beautiful. I was madly in love with him, and he with me. It was an unsettling as well as intoxicating feeling, and I could think of little else but him. We often met in the park before classes, and it was so hard to part from each other that we were late for school and got detention more than once. On my sixteenth birthday he had given me a book in that park, Saint-Exupéry's *The Little Prince.* I still have it.

My new home was a happy home. Mother was happy, and *Batjuschka's* presence was very soothing. I had not realized before what a wonderful sense of humor he had, and the apartment was filled with laughter and good-natured bantering.

Mother took a sales job in a very fancy umbrella shop called *Hugendubel,* where she worked for many years, so we had enough to live on.

Tina had left school the year before and wanted to study art. She was very gifted in drawing, painting, and designing. Father forbade it and got her a position in a department store, where she sold coats. Sometimes she could help with the displays in the windows, but not very often. She was very unhappy.

After the move she changed jobs and worked in a big record store. There she met a young musician, just sixteen years old. He had a Dixieland band and played many different instruments but was phenomenal on the clarinet and trumpet. He became besotted with the older, quietly exotic Tina. When he turned eighteen, they married, but the marriage lasted only a few years. He was irresponsible with money, lied, and had girlfriends on the side. They separated, and Tina went to England to work as an au pair.

Maureen came to stay with us that summer in our new apartment. I took her all over Stuttgart, to various castles and scenic attractions. The highlight of her visit was when we went to an old medieval castle near Rothenburg ob der Tauber, which had been converted into a youth hostel. Our class had spent two weeks there the previous summer on a field study. Below the castle was a small pond, where we could swim and sunbathe. At the local village dance Maureen met a young man, a student whose family owned a large farm nearby. They fell in love, just like that. It was obviously meant to be. They kept in touch and a few years later they got married and moved to Vienna, Austria, where they both worked at the United Nations.

My visit to England had shown me how much freer and less oppressed I could feel in a foreign country. Speaking another language had also freed me to some degree from the past and its associations. German was such a graphic language and often conjured up unwanted images. English was so clear and unencumbered to me. I was determined, more than ever, to leave the country of my birth at the earliest opportunity.

CHAPTER 35

I wish I could pull
My skin over my head,
And hide,
Then die . . .

—Sabina de Werth Neu,
from "Coming Apart" (unpublished poem, 1990)

If it had not been for an event in February of 1958, life for me would have continued to improve all around as it did for most people in West Germany. The long, lean years were over; a new prosperity had spread to most sectors of people's lives, so much so that in Stuttgart we had many guest workers from Italy to help in the reconstruction.

I was sixteen, somewhat sweet, popular at school, and had many friends. I was looking forward to leaving Father and starting a new life with Mother, *Batjuschka*, and Tina later that year. The war years and their aftermath are hazy to me now. I lived in the moment and was consumed by my unsettling but delicious feelings for Frieder, my first real love.

All this changed when in January of that year, Dr. Birk, our Catholic chaplain, invited me to attend a weekend seminar on jazz and religion, as he was aware of my interest. I felt thrilled to be considered mature enough for such a grown-up event. I got there early on Saturday morning and took a seat in the second row, so as not to miss anything. As the auditorium filled, I realized that I was the youngest person there.

The speaker, whom I'll call Dr. Horst Schmidt, was mesmerizing. He was so fluent and at ease as he led the audience through the early history of jazz to the present with countless musical examples. Despite

Sabina and friend Ines, feeling all grown up and ready for the university, 1959

the rudimentary introduction I had received from Mr. Porter, I started to understand the historical and spiritual significance this music held for the people who were forced to come to America as slaves. They mixed the musical elements of their places of origin with the hymns and traditions of their slave masters. What evolved was something quite unique and helped these dispossessed people of Africa to express some of their loss and suffering.

Dr. Schmidt kept making eye contact with me throughout his talk. Blood rushed into my face, and I felt self-conscious and confused. During the break he walked over to me and invited me to have coffee with him. I felt very flattered, but there was another feeling, almost as if all this had been planned, a long time ago. I was swept away by the attention of this educated, secure man, more than twice my age. After the seminar on Sunday, he offered to drive me home, and we stopped in a fancy coffeehouse where he gave me his address in Karlsruhe and various phone numbers so we could stay in touch with each other.

I didn't tell Mother about it, suspecting that she would not approve. Part of me knew it wasn't entirely proper and that I might get into some kind of trouble, even though I did not know what trouble that might be. But I was too star-struck to pay much attention to those thoughts.

He came to Stuttgart twice during the rest of January and invited me to attend two jazz concerts, one with Duke Ellington and his big band; the other with the Modern Jazz Quartet, whom I met after the performance. I had lied to my mother, saying I was going with my friend Ines and her mother to see a late movie. The fact was that I danced in a nightclub with Percy Heath, the quartet's bassist, and sat at the bar drinking my first whiskey. My "friend" drove me home and kissed me good night. It was very different from the way Frieder had kissed me before, a bit frightening and urgent, as well as breathtaking. I did not know what to make of it. Even at sixteen I was very hazy about anything to do with sex; all I knew were just some rumors from classmates. Most of my "sex education" came from movies and books and showed men and women in very romantic situations, just hinting at things.

So Horst and I wrote and phoned each other. In February he sent me a return railway ticket to visit him in Karlsruhe. Ines covered for me, and I took the train there to meet him.

It was late when I arrived, so we went straight to his studio apartment, where he wanted me to hear some of the latest jazz records. It was an amazing place. The walls were filled with shelves housing tens of thousands of record albums, the carpet was white, and there was little furniture but much art and carved masks from all over the world. He had cooked us a simple but nice dinner, after which we sat on the couch, listening to music, drinking American bourbon, and smoking. I was thinking how envious some of my friends would be if they could see me. I felt sophisticated and sure I could handle anything.

After a while my head started to spin, and I felt very tired. I went to the bathroom, while Horst made up a bed for me on the thick carpet, as he had promised. When I returned he picked me up and lowered me onto the pillow and sheet. By now I felt somewhat nauseous. All at once I was being felt up all over, and his heavy body on top of me was making it hard to breathe. I did not like the way he fondled and squeezed my small breasts. I became very scared. I wanted him off me, but no matter how often I said "No, please, no, don't, get off, no," he continued to take my clothes off, including my panties, and then I felt him tearing into me.

It hurt terribly, and suddenly I was back on the farm in the Czech Republic at the mercy of the Russian soldiers. The whole horror of that night crashed over me in full details, details I had not remembered until now. It was all happening again. I was so small and helpless and could only make a faint whimper.

Later when the weight had gone, I sat up. I saw him lying on the couch, snoring. It was a disgusting sight, his flaccid penis lying on his hairy thigh. I got up, my thighs sticky from him and my own blood, and went to the bathroom and cleaned myself up as well as I could. I collected my clothes from the floor, got dressed feverishly, put on my heavy winter coat, took my small bag, and left the apartment.

It was pitch-dark outside and extremely cold. In my haste I had left my gloves and hat behind. I walked toward the railway station, one foot in front of the other, trancelike, trying to put as much distance between me and what had just happened. The station waiting room was open but unheated, the wooden benches hard and pitiless. It was four o'clock in the morning. At five thirty I caught the first train back to Stuttgart.

I don't know which was worse: the rape that had just occurred or the hideous memories of that early time in my childhood, which had suddenly come alive. It seemed all the same, and part of me felt totally numb and filled with a heavy gray hopelessness.

On that train ride back, the enormity of what I had walked into hit me. How could I have been so naive? I had not just lost my physical innocence; I had lost my trust in myself. It was my own fault, my own vanity, that had allowed me to give away my only treasure, my virginity. Without it, I then believed, love, marriage, children, and a normal life were now forever out of reach. I had fallen from grace. The weight of a moral and judging society was crashing down on me. I had failed in every way and brought all this upon myself. At sixteen I should have known better. I was to blame. The shame and guilt I felt was almost unbearable.

Everyone was out when I finally got home. I took a long bath, but the hot water could not wash away the blood-red shame. I staggered through the next few days, pretending to be who I had been before my deflowering. I quickly learned to smile and hide my inner turmoil from everyone, all the while being amazed that nobody noticed the enormous change I had undergone.

So I went through the next few years, outwardly okay, going through the motions and making others laugh with my jokes. I felt so isolated from the world; my sleep was disturbed by nightmares, and flashbacks came at the most unexpected moments. I was anxious, nervous, scared, and no longer had any respect for myself. I drank alcohol whenever I could get some. It brought me a short-lived relief but left me even emptier afterward.

Looking back now, I realize that at that time I nearly went crazy. The need to find something to redeem myself had become overwhelming. I did something that I have never been able to talk about and had nearly forgotten.

I bought a small khaki military shirt from the American PX store, which I turned into an officer's shirt by sewing tiny colored ribbons above the left breast pocket to make them look like decorations. Three brass buttons on each shoulder strap made the shirt look believable, at least to my eyes. I also sewed a knee-length khaki pencil skirt for myself.

Mother was at work during the day, so I could go home after school and change into my "uniform." Then I'd take the tram into the city center of Stuttgart and sit down at a café. There I would sit quite conspicuously, smoking a cigarette over an espresso, and just wait.

I was out "fishing," and my appearance was the bait. And sure enough, I attracted curious men, usually older middle-aged men, who would approach my table and ask to join me. I pretended to speak in broken German so that sooner or later I was questioned about which country I served. That was my moment. I'd respond, "I am working for Mossad, the Israeli secret service," and then watch very closely for the slightest twitch, facial expression, sweaty brow, or any other sign of shock. I was hoping to catch a former Nazi war criminal. It was a real rush, and I felt powerful to think that I might bring a Nazi with a record to justice. I did it only a few times, unsuccessfully, of course.

Now I feel embarrassed writing about it, but I think it shows to what extent I would go to lighten my heavy burden of guilt and shame.

I was still seeing Frieder. Things had gotten more serious, and we started talking about getting married after college. I reluctantly confessed the rape. He wanted to know the man's name so he could go kill him. He was very serious about it and even knew how to get hold of a revolver. I could not tell him, of course. I wanted him to make love to me, hoping it would erase the memory of the rape and make me whole again. But Frieder wouldn't, not before we were married. So eventually, in 1961, we broke up. It was very painful. I made some feeble suicide attempts, hoping that it would somehow make everything turn out all right.

The early sixties were hard and confusing years for me. At least I had passed the *Abitur* and was accepted to Freiburg University. But then I experienced another life-changing event, which radically altered my academic plans.

In my first year I met a sweet, young, sexually experienced student and got pregnant. I didn't feel that we had any future together, so I refused to marry him. In 1962, I gave birth to my daughter, Nicoline. But in my state of mind at the time I couldn't cope with the reality of being a single mother and wanted nothing more than to escape what to me seemed an intolerable situation. So my sister Tina volunteered to look after Nicoline while I went "into exile."

At first, I fled to Greece and Turkey, vowing never to come back again and planning to hitchhike all the way to Tibet, where I dreamed I could live out my ruined life as a Buddhist nun. Looking at it now, I realize it was very melodramatic, but at the time, inside "the windmills of my mind," it seemed the only way out of the mess.

Fortunately, in Istanbul I was persuaded by a German student not to cross into a mostly Muslim Asia. "You'll end up in a harem or get killed, you'll never make it through all these Muslim countries with

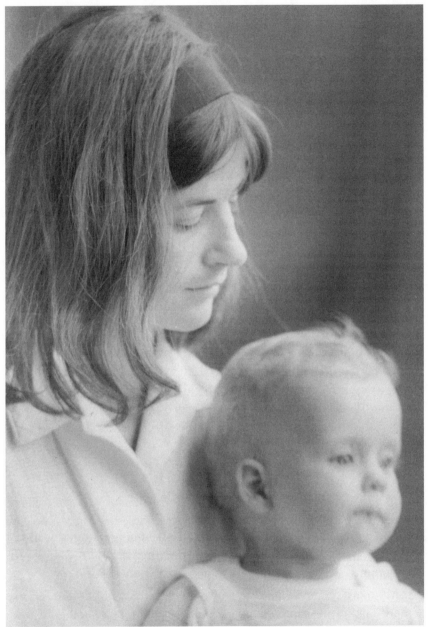

Tina with Sabina's daughter, Nicoline

Sabina, Freiburg, circa 1960

your long blonde hair," was his advice. He gave me the name of a family he had befriended on the island of Crete who lived in a remote village on the southern coast. "Go there and chill out."

That is exactly what I did with just two hundred deutsch marks in my pocket. In the small fishermen's summer village of Matala I met my future husband, a D. H. Lawrence look-alike, who seemed wise and was nonthreatening.

The following fourteen years I spent in England make up an interesting but separate story, better left for another book, perhaps. There my second child, a boy named Simon, was born, and there, too, my abandoned daughter joined us at the age of two. Along with a group of eccentric artists, we joined the craze for self-suffiency, living off the land and bartering wherever possible.

My marriage to Brian turned out to be loveless, and I often felt like a mere shadow in search of my lost self. My depression and guilt were in perfect harmony with the English climate: the frequent rain and the

My future husband, Brian

low-hanging gray clouds. A Mediterranean climate would have finished me off. My children became my lifeline; so did the various gardens I cultivated and created with all the tenderness that would flow out of me periodically and unexpectedly.

Somehow I still functioned. Living in England certainly helped, as did speaking English, despite being referred to as a *Kraut* by Brian and being told not to teach the children any German. His distaste for the Germans was very strong; he was ten years older and remembered the German blitz vividly. This gave me an excuse to completely abandon my past. I remember thinking that I had amputated my former self, left it behind like a severed leg to rot in Germany. I really believed I could disconnect from the past as if it had happened to someone else. I was becoming a master of denial, and the dissociation was nearly successful.

I even gave up the literature and poetry I had loved so much, and for many years I would not read anything in German. Gone were my favorite poets—Rainer Maria Rilke, Heinrich Heine, Johann Wolfgang von Goethe, and the novels of Thomas Mann. The only thing I could hold on to—maybe because there were no words involved—was the music of Bach, Beethoven, Schubert, Mahler, and many others. I did not think of music as just German.

I began to devour the English classics. We had no television, and reading was a great pleasure. Thomas Hardy became my favorite author for a while, and I cried repeatedly over the fate of *Tess of the D'Urbervilles*, with whom I could identify so completely.

I began to believe that I was a survivor. My creativity emerged bit by bit. I started a small business designing and manufacturing leather garments. I joined a fine English choir at Ely Cathedral in the Fen country (north of Cambridge) and rediscovered my passion for singing. I met some wonderful Americans, and my dream of going to live in America was resurrected.

I was back on track; I had survived up until now, and I could and would make my dream come true at last. From 1975 to 1977 I worked with great determination to get immigration visas for the four of us. Despite many setbacks, we were finally allowed to come to America, as legal aliens (this time *we* were from another planet), clutching our green cards.

On March 27, 1977, at the age of thirty-five, and twenty-eight years after first experiencing the kindness of the American soldiers outside my elementary school in Germany, I stepped onto American soil in Boston, Massachusetts, from a British Airways plane. For me it was as triumphant as if I had landed at Plymouth Rock on the *Mayflower*.

Within the first twenty-four hours, in our new house in Newport, Rhode Island, I started to make the connection to my former self. The next morning I looked out the window to view the bluest sky and most brilliant sunshine I had seen in a long time, while a huge robin was trilling outside. I stepped outdoors in my nightie. Everything was in Technicolor; the air smelled of the ocean, birds were singing, and all my senses were reawakened. But most of all I felt physically safe for the first time in my life. America was so far away from the Soviet missiles threatening the whole of Europe.

Just arrived in America, 1977

I found myself in the place I had longed to visit for so many years, my "America the Beautiful," the land from which I had been loved and cared for as a child. I was welcomed and accepted with love and openness to share this land in all its breathtaking beauty. I was home at last—the home of my larger-than-life Uncle Marshall.

Our family, first two weeks in the USA

241

AFTERWORD

For the last few months I have had a recurring dream. I am walking on a frozen lake where I see parts of pale bodies under the ice, half hidden by thin layers of drifting snow.

The other night I was back in the dream; the snow had blown away, and there under the ice was my mother, preserved perfectly. Next to her were my two sisters, and a little over to one side, I saw the adolescent body of myself. I tried to break the thin ice with my brittle fingernails, desperate to save us.

I woke up in tears and was filled with an indescribable sadness. The image was the truth; we had indeed been frozen in our different ways, in our silence, which was louder and more powerful than our talking, singing, or trying to carry on a normal life had ever been.

Like so many Germans, we had allowed ourselves—as if by agreement—to be wrapped in a cloak of deafening silence about our recent national history as well as our own personal stories. There were really no adequate words for what had happened, and to bemoan our own fate seemed totally inappropriate, even arrogant.

I wish that my sister Tina was still alive and could have taken part in the dialogue that finally started in the eighties and is still going on. Her loathing for Nazi Germany and her own self-recriminations for even being alive made her flee to England as I had. She, too, felt better in a foreign country with a new language.

She had brought me my two-year-old Nicoline and stayed in London with a friend. She decided to become a teacher and went to college. Thereafter, she volunteered to work in one of the most neglected areas of southeast London and taught mostly immigrant children from Pakistan, India, Uganda, and the British West Indies. She could pour all her love and compassion into being a safe haven and support to these uprooted, skinny, and often shy children, who must have reminded her of her own young self.

But it was too much for her; she burned out after two years and had to give it up. By then, she had met a young man named Pat, a computer genius who spoke in whispers and had no edges, no definition. I never heard him express any opinion about anything. Tina married him just because he was so pliable and nonthreatening. She despised masculine or assertive men.

Pat was a good provider. The two of them referred to themselves as PATINA, as if neither one of them wanted a defined identity. Tina apprenticed to restore pottery at the British Museum. She had wonderfully creative hands and had made exquisite pottery while at college. She seemed settled at last. Pat won an international competition and accepted an invitation to go to Saudi Arabia to create computer programs in Arabic script that could easily be converted into other languages—a big thing in the 1970s.

Tina studied Arabic with great enthusiasm and learned to write it beautifully. She and Pat lived in Riyadh for several years. There she fell in love, for the very first time, with a young artist from Egypt. It must all have been very dramatic, like in *Anna Karenina*, only without a child, of course. After two very serious suicide attempts, of which we knew nothing at the time, she left for London, where she got a flat in the very depressed southeast section.

Her lover from Egypt, Zamir, came to visit. But what had worked in Saudi Arabia did not work in London. Zamir returned to Cairo. I know all this from some tortured poetry I found after Tina's death.

Pat returned to London in 1981 and asked for a divorce. He wanted to marry a young girl whom he had gotten pregnant. That was the last straw for Tina. When they were still PATINA, she had her tubes tied so she could never bear a child. She strongly believed it was immoral to bring new life into this rotten world. She felt betrayed and angry.

AFTERWORD

She had planned her death several months before, graduating from the Hemlock Society (a national right-to-die organization) in order to do it right this time. Tina had considered suicide to be an option since her teenage years. This time, she feverishly prepared for it, writing us all wonderful last letters that were filled with joy and love, nothing in them to foreshadow what was about to happen. She mailed them all on the morning of her last day, October 28, 1981.

I was away on a sailing trip and did not get my letter until two weeks later. I remember turning over the envelope and reading the printed label: "I have no home, only a PO box. Visit me there." I did not get it. The letter was lovely, telling me how much she loved me.

Then the phone rang. I can still hear my mother's voice: "Tina is dead; she has already been cremated!" She told me three times while I was shouting, "No, no, I don't believe it!" I hung up and dialed Tina's number in London. The number had been disconnected. I tried again and again. I called Mother, and she had to tell me everything she knew. We cried together; oh, how we cried.

She had ended her fragile life to Bach's Cantata BWV 82, *Ich Habe Genug* (I Have Enough). The music was playing on a continuous loop when her doctor entered her apartment through the unlocked door as instructed by her letter delivered that afternoon. She was thoughtful and considerate to the very end.

After nearly twenty-six years, my vulnerable sister Tina still appears in my dreams. She has left a large empty space in my soul.

Gabi, the oldest, received the security she so badly needed at the time when she married Peter, a radiologist by profession. She has spent her entire life with this man, who turned out to be mean and destructive. She was not allowed to have any friends of her own or to come and visit me; only once after Tina's death could I persuade him to let her come to America. He had lost his own sixty-year-old mother to suicide, to escape her despot of a husband. Peter is a chip off the old block.

But Gabi's life has some new happiness at last, two young grandchildren. Unfortunately, Peter has developed mental problems in recent years.

AFTERWORD

He is acting paranoid and will not allow anyone to come to their house or premises—no repairmen, gardeners, not even a cleaning lady. As a result, their villa with a million-dollar view is deteriorating and dirty; even the toilets are barely functioning after decades of neglect. I feel sad for Gabi. She is all I have left now. Real contact is all but impossible.

Tante Marga stayed married to her Otto and had a comfortable life. Emotionally, she was very closed off despite her outward charm. You never knew how she really felt. Both are gone now.

My father tried to make all sorts of trouble for me while I was at Freiburg University in the early sixties after he found out that I had had a baby. I had been on a scholarship, and he had nothing better to do than to see my professor and tell him how depraved I was. Professor Hess threw him out of his office, telling him that he was not a fit father and did not deserve a daughter like me. That was one of the nicest things anybody had done for me.

About six months later, on Monday, May 12, 1963, I got a telegram from Mother. It read: "Father dead—stop—massive heart attack—stop—it is over—stop—*Mutti*." I do not apologize for being elated. He had done so many mean things. I felt no sense of loss, only relief. I got some friends together and invited them for a beer in our favorite hangout near the *Münster* (cathedral). It was a sunny, good day.

When *Batjuschka* died, the day was sunny too, but heavy with grief. I got the news by phone in late June of 1979 that he was very ill. I raced up to Boston from Newport to get on the Lufthansa evening flight to Frankfurt. The flight was completely full. I was in tears. I had to see my (real) father before it was too late, I explained. A total stranger stepped up: "Give this young lady my seat; I can fly tomorrow." I was too emotional to get his phone number to thank him adequately later for his incredible kindness.

By the time I arrived in Stuttgart, *Batjuschka* had died. Peritonitis had set in, and the second emergency operation was too much for his seventy-eight-year-old heart. Mother was in total shock, and I held her for hours. The next day a very subdued Tina flew in from Riyadh; she was frighteningly thin and felt cold after the desert heat.

Mother nearly went to pieces. She was unable to grasp that their life together could have come to such a sudden stop. She appeared much smaller and older, as if the structure inside her had collapsed. But in the next few weeks the memory of their many happy years together propped her upright like invisible crutches.

She relived the last twenty years and the wonderful project they had both thrown all their energy and passion into. They had purchased a small three-hundred-year-old granite-stone house high above the village of Mergoscia, in the Ticino region of Switzerland, above the Lago Maggiore. The little summer house, which Mother called a *Hütte* (hut), was very primitive; there was no electricity or running water, and only narrow paths led up to it. It had been built into the steep slope and was used by the local people during the summer.

Mother's Swiss mountain "hut"

AFTERWORD

John and Mother in their mountain paradise.

The lower part had been for the goats and maybe one milk cow; it had a large door made of chestnut wood and a small slit in the stone wall for ventilation. The second floor had held the hay, and there was a small flagstone area with a fireplace, which served as a shelter.

With the help of a wonderful old man named Lorenzo Cadra, the *capanna al ciliego* (small house at the cherry tree) was transformed into a jewel of a mountain cabin. Windows were installed; the inside was paneled with pine wood to keep small animals out (which could come through the cracks in the stones), and the rafters were strengthened to hold the granite slabs that formed the roof. Some water from a spring farther up the mountain was diverted in plastic pipes, and a toilet and outdoor sink were built.

Planning, buying things, and getting it all up the mountain were the first major steps; sewing curtains and seat cushions followed. Finally, when the preliminaries were nearly complete, furniture, a woodstove, and more were flown up by helicopter. All this took up many summers and kept Mother in a constant state of excitement and creativity. I believe it prolonged her life.

The *capanna* was the first house she had ever owned and her first piece of land; it included birch and sweet chestnut trees, huge boulders, wildflowers, butterflies, and emerald lizards. And it was all in Switzerland, a neutral country not touched by war and safe from the Soviet Union. Mother had finally found a safe haven. *Batjuschka* also learned to love their little paradise, despite being an ocean person. He became an expert tree cutter and wood splitter and took great pride in stacking his harvest.

Mother planned and collected things all winter, and in late spring she and John were back in the Ticino, ready to spend the long summer up in their refuge. They carried large backpacks with provisions and other small necessities. Local villagers would walk up with produce from their gardens, milk, fresh eggs, and so on. The villagers developed a great admiration for these two elderly Germans who had such determination and love for the place they themselves took for granted. They started to see their familiar valley with new eyes, and many who owned *capannas*, dotted around the mountain, started to make theirs habitable and come up on weekends to enjoy their new vacation homes.

Those years with *Batjuschka* in their mountain retreat were the happiest in Mother's life. I would visit her most summers, arriving by boat and train from London, sometimes with the children.

After *Batjuschka*'s and Tina's deaths, I would mostly come alone. Sadly, I often found Mother depressed when I got there; she was alone too much. The villagers came up rarely now, as they, too, were getting old, and their offspring had no interest in the simple life, preferring to go down to Locarno on their mopeds. But Mother stuck it out for another ten summers; she was not about to give up her sanctuary. It had been more effective than all the therapy she had had over the years. She took her periodic bouts of depression stoically, knowing they would eventually lift and she would be herself again for a while.

But after Tina's death, Mother wasn't herself anymore; she even denied that my sister had ever existed. That was the only way her mind

AFTERWORD

My mother on the terrace of her Swiss mountain retreat

could handle the loss. She often called my daughter Tina and could no longer refer to anything more than twenty years in the past.

Nicoline, by that time living in Germany, became a great comfort to her. She now carries on the tradition, together with my nephew Stephan, and spends all her vacation time in what is now her retreat.

Frieder, my first boyfriend, became a doctor. He came down with Parkinson's disease in his forties and is cared for by his loving and patient wife. We have kept up a wonderful friendship over the years. He and some of my old friends are the only bridge I have to my early years. It feels as if they have held onto me with an invisible silver thread through time.

I wish I could have seen my mother while she was still alive as I see her now, after writing these reminiscences. I wish I could have talked to her and thanked her for having been such a fighter and for saving our lives. All I can do now is send her an imaginary letter:

AFTERWORD

To my Mother, Klarissa:

   I see you now, all of you: the girl, graceful and full of hope; the woman, sad and yet proud; the mother, kind and so scared. I am because of you; I dance because of you; I live because of you; I weep for war and you. You gave me life; you are still giving it. Every day when I pause, for just a moment, in that place where you no longer are, in that hole in my heart that you have filled with endless gifts, I pick one: Some days I discover again a brief glimpse of your profile under a wide-brimmed hat, or three bars of a Chopin ballade; on another day it is a gesture of delight from your expressive hands. You are long gone; for fifteen years I have lived without you. I have loved; I have danced; I have wept. Only now can I truly thank you for being who you were and still are in me. I see you now; I finally see you now!

Sabina

Sabina and husband, Charles E. Neu

AFTERWORD

But sixteen years ago I was still struggling with my own personal past, learning to forgive myself for my own shortcomings. I was also playing catch-up with the early adulthood I had somehow missed. I had to learn a lot about dating and the complexities of relationships after I finally divorced Brian, my English husband. I found an excellent therapist in California who helped me to gain a different perspective on life. That is where the healing started.

After my return to the East Coast, I went back to school and finished my degrees, then started my own counseling practice. I met my current husband, Charles, whose lightness of being together with his depth of understanding, sense of humor, and beautiful mind literally swept me away. Maybe only a modern historian could have given me the respect and empathy for all that has formed me. The last thirteen years have been an unexpected and precious gift. Through Charles's love for me I found the courage to write this memoir.

So many civilians in wartime have suffered much more than our family. In many ways we were the lucky ones. Many of them cannot tell their stories of rape, torture, degradation, bomb attacks, and witnessing the unspeakable barbarisms that occur in war. I think it is important to tell our stories whenever and however we can, for our own survival and for a greater understanding of the horrendous effects of war everywhere. Will it make nations think before they go to war? I do not know and dare not hope when I look at what is happening in the world right now.

But we have to try. Silence is not an option any longer.

TIMELINE

1933	Hitler elected German chancellor.
February	My maternal grandfather, Arthur Maskus, head of the German Freethinker Organization, is murdered by Nazi thugs.
May 3	My mother, Klarissa Maskus, marries my father, Bernd de Werth.
1934	More than a thousand opponents assassinated, others removed. All powers of state go to Hitler. Nazi Party becomes official party; all others are banned.
1935	Compulsory military service, air force rebuilt, and general rearmament.
	My sister Gabriele (Gabi) is born.
1936	Hitler forms alliance with Mussolini of Italy.
1938	Hitler appoints himself commander of armed forces. Alliance with Japan. Occupation of Austria. Preparations for the invasion of Czechoslovakia.
	The *Kristallnacht* (Night of Broken Glass) starts a nationwide program against all Jews. Propaganda war against Great Britain.
	My sister Kristina (Tina) is born.
1939	German troops occupy Czechoslovakia. Authorization to kill all people of Polish descent or language. Nonaggression agreement with Russia.
	Britain and Poland sign common Defense Pact.
Sept. 1	Germany invades Poland. **Start of World War II.**
Sept. 3	Britain, France, and Austria declare war on Germany, as does Canada.

	Heavy losses by Poland as Red Army invades from the east. Poland falls. Soviets attack Finland.
1940	Mighty offensive by Hitler in Europe called the *Blitzkrieg* (lightning war).
	German troops invade Denmark, which has to surrender, then Norway, which resists with British and French help for a while, but has to surrender eventually. By May the Germans have taken the Netherlands, Belgium, and Luxemburg. German planes bomb Paris. French planes bomb Berlin, Frankfurt, and Munich.
	Italy declares war on Allies. Australia and New Zealand declare war on Italy. Britain prepares for German invasion. Air raids over London and elsewhere, Battle of Britain in the air.
	Night raids over Berlin by the Royal Air Force.
1941	By 1941 Germany with its Axis partners occupies Czechoslovakia, Poland, Lithuania, Latvia, Estonia (the latter two were captured by the Soviets later), and the western Soviet Union, in the West, half of France, Belgium, the Netherlands, Luxemburg, Denmark, Norway, Yugoslavia, Albania, Greece, Austria, Hungary, Romania, Bulgaria, Italy, and Libya. The only neutral countries left are Sweden and Switzerland.
	By June more than one hundred divisions of armed Germans and Axis partners (approx. 1,750,000 men) are poised along the Soviet borders. Stalin quickly changes his alliance to Britain. Bad weather and mud make fighting very difficult and there are defeats in both Moscow and Stalingrad.
Sept. 26	I am born in Berlin.
Dec. 7	Japanese attack Pearl Harbor and declare war on the United States and Britain.
Dec. 8	The United States, Britain, and Australia declare war on Japan.

TIMELINE

Dec. 10	Germany and Italy declare war on the United States.
Dec. 11	The United States returns the favor.
	Russia starts pushing back German forces. Hitler orders "no withdrawal."
1942	For nine more months, the German army pushes back into Soviet territory.
	Our father, on leave from the German *Luftwaffe* (air force), visits my mother, my sisters, and me in Berlin.
January	Start of "Final Solution," all Jews to be transported to the east, worked to death, and the remainder put to death.
	Mother, my sisters, and I, along with our nanny, Hertha, are forced to evacuate Berlin and move to the small village of Rundfliess south of Königsberg, East Prussia (today Kaliningrad, Russia).
September	Final German offensive at Stalingrad.
November	Soviets push Germans back. The decline of expansion starts.
1942–43	Occasional visits from *Onkel* Kurt, now an officer on the eastern front.
1943	Last major offensive on Russian front.
November	Royal Air Force begins "Battle of Berlin."
1944	Royal Air Force bombings continue.
January	Red Army crosses Polish frontiers. The 900-day blockade of Leningrad is lifted.
June	D-Day, Allies land on Normandy Beach. Anglo and American bombers inflict terrible destruction on German cities, especially Dresden. Red Army advances.
July 20	Assassination attempt on Hitler at his East Prussian hideout Rastenberg, by Colonel Claus von Stauffenberg.
October	We are forced to flee westward from East Prussia, as the Red Army invades German territory. We get as far as a small village near Zwittau (now Svitavy) in the Czech Republic.
November	*Onkel* Kurt is reported missing in battle and is never found.

TIMELINE

1945   Allies liberate concentration camps, between January and April.

Apr. 12   FDR dies, Truman sworn in.

Apr. 30   Hitler commits suicide with Eva Braun. Bodies are burnt. Tens of thousands of German civilians are still trying to escape the fury of the Red Army.

May 8   **Germany's unconditional surrender.**
                Marauding Soviet troops storm through our village and attack civilians, including my mother, sisters, and me.

July   We are forcibly expelled from Zwittau in the Czech Republic and shipped west to Gera, Thuringia, East Germany.

Aug. 6   Nuclear bombs dropped on Hiroshima and Nagasaki, Japan.

Aug. 14   Japan surrenders.

Sept. 4   Formal surrender by Japan and **official end of World War II.**
                The civilian death count has been reported to be as many as 73 million.

November   Nuremburg trials begin. Top Nazis and SS personnel who committed the atrocities in the concentration camps are imprisoned and many are executed by hanging.
                Potsdam Conference divides Germany into four military zones, British, French, American, and Soviet. Land in the east given to Poland and Russia. Prussia is abolished, expulsion of all remaining Germans. Many die.

1945–46   German population on near starvation level.

1946   In the fall, Mother decides we must all move west to get out of the Soviet occupation zone. We flee at night on a train and wind up in a Red Cross refugee camp near Bebra. The Red Cross locates our father in Stuttgart. We move there.

1947   Under leadership of President Truman, the Marshall Plan is instituted, to stabilize Europe with aid.

TIMELINE

Spring	We are allocated two rooms in a villa in the suburb of Degerloch.
1948	I enter first grade. I encounter the American army for the first time when they come to school to serve the students hot lunch.
1949	The Federal Republic of Germany is formed, known as West Germany. In the east the German Democratic Republic is established under the Soviets and becomes a Communist State. NATO, an alliance of Western powers, is formed to protect the West from Soviet expansionism, leading to the "Cold War," with two ideologies facing each other.
1950	I am sent to the Austrian Alps to be "fattened up" courtesy of the Marshall Plan.
Fall	Our family begins receiving CARE packages from the United States.
1951	In the spring, I start *Gymnasium* in Degerloch and begin studying English, drama, and other subjects.
1953	Stalin dies. The Marshall Plan is funneling huge loans into West Germany to rebuild the country, leading to prolonged economic growth, later known as the *Wirtschaftswunder* (economic miracle).
Summer	We move to a new apartment in Bad Cannstatt.
Sept.	I begin attending the girls *Gymnasium* in Bad Cannstatt.
1954	At school we have to watch a film documenting in graphic detail the German atrocities against the Jews during the war.
Spring	Mother meets John Weitzenberg, commencing a romance that eventually leads to divorce from my father and marriage to John (Batjuschka).
1955	Germany is allowed to join NATO. East Germany is struggling. Many flee across the border to the West; many are shot trying to escape.

TIMELINE

	The Berlin Wall is erected, cutting the city in half. It becomes a symbol of the Cold War.
Spring	I attend school for two weeks on an American military base.
August	I spend a month in a state children's home in Rot an der Rot near Lake Constance to improve my health.
1957	In August I visit my English pen pal, Maureen Lawrence, in Broadstairs, Kent.
April	Mother divorces father and marries John.
1961	I enroll in Freiburg University.
1962	My daughter, Nicoline, is born.
1963	In May, my father dies of a massive heart attack. I marry Brian, an Englishman, and move to England.
1964	My son, Simon, is born.
1977	Our family emigrates to the United States.
1979	Batuschka dies.
1981	Tina dies.
1984	I divorce Brian.
1989	With the collapse of the Soviet Union, the Berlin Wall is torn down by the people.
1990	East Germany is reunited with West Germany.
1992	Mother dies.
1998	I get a master's degree in counseling.
1999	I marry Charles E. Neu.
2006	I begin writing *A Long Silence*.